Unraveled

Also by

Maria Housden

———

Hannah's Gift

Unraveled

One Woman's Story of Moving Out,
Moving On, and Becoming a
Different Kind of Mother

Maria Housden

THREE RIVERS PRESS
NEW YORK

Grateful acknowledgment is made to W. W. Norton & Company, Inc., for
permission to reprint excerpts from "The Layers." Copyright © 1978 by
Stanley Kunitz, from *Passing Through: The Later Poems New
and Selected* by Stanley Kunitz. Reprinted by permission of
W. W. Norton & Company, Inc.

www.crownpublishing.com

Three Rivers Press and the Tugboat design are registered trademarks of
Random House, Inc.

Originally published in Great Britain by
Element Books, London, in 2004.

Subsequently published in hardcover in the United States by Harmony
Books, an imprint of the Crown Publishing Group, a division of Random
House, Inc., New York, in 2005.

Library of Congress Cataloging-in-Publication Data
Housden, Maria.
Unraveled : one woman's story of moving out, moving on, and becoming a
better mother / Maria Housden.—1st ed.
   1. Divorced mothers.   2. Divorced people—Family relationships.
   3. Children of divorced parents—Family relationships.   I. Title.
         HQ814.H74   2005
     306.89'3—dc22   2004020034

ISBN-13: 978-1-4000-5417-6
ISBN-10: 1-4000-5417-6

Printed in the United States of America

Design by Lynne Amft

10 9 8 7 6 5 4 3 2 1

First Paperback Edition

In memory of my beloved father,
Ronald Guy Schlack

CONTENTS

vii

THE LAYERS

I have walked through many lives,

some of them my own,

and I am not who I was,

though, some principle of being

abides, from which I struggle

not to stray. . . .

"Live in the layers,

not on the litter."

Though I lack the art

to decipher it,

no doubt the next chapter

in my book of transformations

is already written.

I am not done with my changes.

Stanley Kunitz

AUTHOR'S NOTE

THE BEST DECISIONS we make in our lives are often the most difficult ones. When I chose to give primary custody of my children to their father, my ex-husband, at the time of our divorce, I had no way of knowing what was around the bend. But I knew that my decision came from a place of deep trust and acceptance of life itself, with all its uncertainties and glory. Today, as a result, I am a changed woman, not because I no longer care about those I love or about how my choices adversely affect others, but because I know our greatest gift as women, as mothers, is not to try to avoid the consequences of our actions or even to try to minimize them. Our greatest gift is our willingness to live our lives with the courage to test our boundaries, to dive ever deeper into uncharted waters, to see how much more fully we can love and live. This is my story.

Unraveled

THE QUOTATION MARKS positioned around the story are intentional, an offering to the way all our stories are simply one version of what happened, no better or worse, truer or less true, than anyone else's memory or recollection.

Prologue

Summer of '75

"AT THE AGE OF TWELVE, I wrote the story of my life. The words flowed effortlessly onto the page; I knew everything then.

My sister Diana and I were leaning against the trunk of the maple tree that marked the dividing line between our backyard and the neighbor's next door. It was early August, a week before my thirteenth birthday; Diana was two years younger than me. We were bored and sweating in the heat, streaks of dirt creased into the backs of our knees and under our chins. I was wearing the same shorts and T-shirt I had worn the past few days, and my canvas tennis shoes, which had been bright white at the beginning of the summer, were now scuffed and gray. Diana drew circles with a stick in the dirt, and I waved half-heartedly at our younger sister and brother, who were riding their bikes up and down the alley with a pack of neighborhood kids, whooping and hollering each time they passed.

The two of us sat in the middle of a circle of limp white string that was tied to wooden stakes our father had erected in an attempt to keep us off the grass he was trying to grow in the only shady part of the yard. Our father was nothing if not disciplined and persistent. Working long hours as a janitorial supply salesman during the week and as a member of the Air Force Reserves on weekends, his scant bit of free time was spent seeding and reseeding patches of dirt. Even so, our yard was mostly dusty sand, a constant parade of bicycles and endless games of Kick the Can crushing any hope of a lawn taking root.

Our house was one of the smallest on the block. It was painted gray on one side, white on the other. Years ago, someone had started painting it and never finished. My parents rented it from Mr. Nyland, a stocky, good-humored man who lived in a bigger house across the street with his wife and teenage kids. Our neighborhood was a midwestern mix of hardworking middle-class families and those who were significantly less hardworking. The most scandalous thing to happen so far that year, besides the juvenile detention of the boy next door for "borrowing" his aunt's car, was the impending divorce of my friend Anne's parents. Her father, a doctor, had been having an affair with one of his nurses. All the mothers in the neighborhood spoke in hushed whispers about it. Nothing, however, was said to us kids.

"I'm bored," Diana said, flinging her stick across the yard.

I tipped my head back and squinted into the sun.

"Boring is what summer is," I said. "At least until we're grown-ups," I added, thinking about our mother, who was inside the house, stretched out on the couch in front of the fan, a cool washcloth folded neatly over her forehead. "When we're grown-ups, we'll be able to do anything we want."

"Yeah, as long as we don't die of boredom first. My butt's even falling asleep," Diana said.

"Hey, wait here," I said, standing up and brushing off the back of my shorts. "I have an idea."

I was careful to be quiet as I let myself into the house. Mom didn't like us kids traipsing in and out, banging the bent screen door. I tiptoed upstairs to my dad's office, which was set up in the corner of my parents' bedroom, just down the hall from my brother's room and the one we three girls shared. I opened the bottom drawer of my dad's desk and lifted a stack of blank typing paper out of the folder in the back. I found two pencil stubs in the pencil holder my brother had made the previous Christmas out of an empty soup can and pieces of felt.

Diana was still sitting in the shady "no-man's-land" when I returned.

"Here's what we're going to do," I said, handing half the paper and a pencil to her. "We're going to write letters to each other as if we're already grown up. You tell me about your life, and I'll tell you about mine."

"How old should we be?" Diana asked, getting into the game.

"Oh, old enough to have everything we want, but not too old to enjoy it. You be thirty-four and I'll be thirty-six," I said.

I leaned back against the trunk of the tree and closed my eyes. The image of what I saw is as clear to me now as it was then. I began writing.

> *Dear Diana,*
>
> *My life is perfect. My husband James and I are happily married. We met when I was an architect just out of college, the year I published my first book. James is a wonderful man, a banker, tall and handsome with black curly hair, twinkling blue eyes and large, strong hands. We live on a horse ranch in the mountains outside Denver, Colorado, just the two of us with our twelve kids.*
>
> *Our children are growing so fast. Justin, the oldest, is already 12. The twins, Elizabeth and Anastasia, are 10, John is 9, Rebecca and Christian are 8, Emily is 7, Ben is 6, Julia and Molly are 4, Thomas is 3, and Sarah is 1. As you can imagine, they keep me very busy. I have time for myself though, too. I love to go horseback riding in*

the mountains, paint, write, or play tennis during the day. At night, James and I often go to fancy restaurants with our friends.

Our family lives in a lovely old Victorian mansion that's painted blue with white gingerbread trim. It has a large porch that goes all the way around the house, and bedrooms for each of our kids. A swing hangs from the branches of a tree in the front yard, and in the back there's a playhouse with lace curtains in the windows, barns with chickens and goats, and a rolling, green horse pasture.

Despite the demands of our busy household, I am able to manage everything quite effortlessly. I love my life, and feel lucky to be the woman I am, the mother of twelve beautiful children, and James's wife.

I hope your life is wonderful too, and that you will be coming to visit us here soon.

Love,
Maria

As I reread my letter before handing it over to my sister, I felt warm and quiet inside. I loved this woman I imagined I would become, this capable, vibrant, sexy, beautiful wife and mother. I knew that her toes were manicured, her purse well organized, and her children neatly dressed and polite. I loved her life, the wholeness and fullness, joy and satisfaction in it.

I felt as if great things were possible for me, things that felt real and familiar even though there was no evidence of them in the life I was now living. I was a secret being kept hidden until the time was right, ripening and waiting for the external world to change before I could be revealed. Sitting beneath the maple tree in our backyard, I felt a deep quiet in the center of myself as I imagined this woman I would become, as if it were already done, as if it were already true for me.

Each of us, in the most silent part of ourselves, has always known who we are. The eyes that look into ours from the image in the mirror recognize something that does not change with time or age. It would take me twenty-four more years to spiral into this center of myself, to discover and begin fully living the sense of happiness and possibility that I dreamed for myself when I was twelve. And in the process, I would have to learn to be fiercely honest with myself and with others, and to unravel, with integrity and discernment, all my ideas about the way *life is supposed to be.*

PART ONE

Ten Days—Ten Years

Summer 1998

SUNDAY

THE ONLY LIGHT in the room came from a single kerosene lamp. I ran my hand along the wall beside the wide-plank door, found a switch, and flicked it on. A copper lamp with a fringed shade made a circle of light on the small wooden table next to the bed. I stood in the center of the room and felt a sense of excitement growing in me. Although I had dreamed of this moment for years, envisioned this place many times before, I hadn't ever truly believed it would happen. Looking around now, anything felt possible, as if something new was coming alive in me, a sense without form, poised to take shape.

The idea of a retreat had been planted in my heart in the first months after Hannah's death. Holding her lifeless body in my arms, part of me had released itself; something in me had irreparably changed. I had known then that I would have to get away, to immerse myself in a silence that was only mine, if I were to ever understand fully what had happened, if I were ever to know what I was supposed to do next.

The Hermitage, the center where I was now staying, had been established years ago by an elderly Mennonite couple who had converted a huge barn into several floors of small bedrooms, libraries, and a kitchen–dining room. For a modest fee, guests were given their own rooms and bath and encouraged to spend their days quietly on their own, reading, painting, writing, or walking in the fields and surrounding woods. All meals, except for breakfast, were prepared by Mary and served to guests around the farm table in silence. It seemed the perfect space for my retreat.

Now, gazing around the room, I felt as if I had been transported into another, timeless place, far from any life I had ever known. The walls were paneled with knotted pine boards that climbed horizontally to the beamed ceiling. Two screened windows on wide hinges were open to the warm summer evening, their white lace curtains catching the breeze. A well-worn plank floor was partially covered by a brown braid rug, and along one wall, facing the largest window, was a double bed with a carved, wooden headboard and muted patchwork quilt. A small teddy bear with button eyes and suede paws leaned against the pillow.

Unraveled

I laid my suitcase on the bed and began to unpack. I stacked my folded clothes in the drawers of the simple bureau, placed my new journal alongside a silver pen on the small desk that sat beneath the window across from the bed, and slid several photographs of my husband, Claude, and our four children, Will, ten; Hannah, who would have been seven; Margaret, three; and Madelaine, two, under the edges of the window frame above. In the drawers of the desk I put pages of drawing paper, a few pencils, and a deck of cards.

Beneath the second window, next to the dresser, was a small kneeling bench with a wooden shelf nailed to the wall above it. Here I placed a votive candle and the gold cross I wore around my neck during the last year of Hannah's life. When I had finished, I slid my suitcase under the bed and sat down in the large, upholstered reading chair in the corner. From my vantage point, I could see fireflies blinking in the dark outside the windows. I sat quietly, not moving, feeling myself breathe.

Mary, the caretaker, had told me when I checked in that one other guest was scheduled to arrive in a day or two; other than that, I would be on my own. Having shared a room with two younger sisters until I was eighteen, and never having lived on my own, the idea of so much solitude and silence seemed too good to be true. And, as a wife and mother, I had become so acclimated to constant interruptions that I couldn't help thinking now that this peaceful feeling couldn't possibly last.

Sitting in the light of the flickering lamp, I heard a rustling noise, just outside the window, and felt a shiver up my spine, suddenly frightened of being alone. Quickly I stood up and, with a running start, leaped across the floor onto the bed, just as I had as a little girl, afraid of monsters that lurked in dark corners. Undressing beneath the covers, I dropped my clothes onto the floor and burrowed beneath the soft sheets and thick quilt. Closing my eyes against the dark and silence, I fell almost immediately into a deep sleep.

Winter 1988

SLIP, SLIDING AWAY

MY BODY WAS NOT MY OWN; *every pore was yawning open. Even the air particles felt charged with anticipation, poised for what was about to happen. The nurse, standing on one side of the bed, was anchoring my foot in the stirrup. Claude, his eyes wild with excitement, held one of my outstretched hands in his.*

The whole of my life, twenty-five years, I had known this moment was coming with the same sense of certainty in which we draw our next breath. What I did not know was whether this baby, my first child, was going to be a boy or a girl. Claude and I had chosen to be surprised at the moment of our baby's birth. I felt grateful, in this breath between contractions, for the sense of excitement I felt, already loving this little person so wholly and completely without knowing for certain whether this baby was a Hannah or a Will.

The next contraction gripped my body, and all my attention was sucked into the sensation as I felt the weight in my pelvis bear down. I imagined the muscles around my cervix expanding and lengthening, the head of the baby, our baby, being pushed through. Dr. Menon, a petite, Indian woman, smiled encouragingly from between my legs at the foot of the bed.

"You're doing great," she murmured softly. "Once this contraction subsides, I'll hold the mirror up so you can see the baby's head."

I nodded briefly, consumed by the intensity of the crescendo running through my body as I tried to remember to breathe. Gradually, almost imperceptibly, the grip of the contraction released and my attention returned to what was happening in the room. Everyone got busy in the pause. The nurse helped the doctor position the mirror between my legs. Claude asked, "Do you want some more ice chips, honey? Is there anything you need?"

"No, just keep holding my hand. I'm doing fine as long as I know you're there."

I had barely exhaled the last word when the next contraction began. It rose like a tsunami from the center of my body. Relentlessly, it rolled outward into the whole of my awareness, swallowing any separate sense of myself. I gave myself to it— opening, offering, and surrendering. Leaning forward, aware of nothing but sensation, I saw in the mirror my swollen, bulging vagina, impossibly stretched around a protruding, dark orb. Dr. Menon took my left hand and placed it gently on the wetness between my legs.

"That," she whispered, *"is your baby's head."*

Some part of me, silently watching, suddenly woke up. As my fingers lightly caressed the slippery softness, the being who until now had been an inherent part of my self and my body became in this moment its own separate person, touching me with its own, slippery head!

I took a deep breath and bore down again, feeling the burn as my perineum tore. *"Breathe,"* the nurse reminded me in a loud voice. I pulled myself away from the center of my body just long enough to expand my lungs and inhale another breath. I screwed up my face and bore down again. *"Relax your face!"* The nurse spoke more loudly. I had never experienced such fullness in any moment; so many things were happening in my body and my awareness that it took everything I had to bring my attention to any single thing.

Then it happened. The intensely concentrated pressure pushing out from the center of my body shifted slightly and began to slide. As the outer lips of my vagina became an expanding ring of fire around the baby's head, Dr. Menon leaned in, closer to my body, and the nurse lifted the mirror out of the way.

"One more push, Maria. Make it a strong, good one," she said.

Claude gripped my hand more tightly and turned his gaze from my face toward what was happening between my legs. I opened my mouth, inhaled a huge breath, closed my lips around it, and bore down. I felt as if my body was being forced through my legs, outside of itself. In the moments before this one, when I had tried to imagine the moment of my baby's birth, I always imagined my eyes closed as I concentrated on the last push. Instead, they remained fully open, allowing everything: the ring of fire, Claude's anxious face, the sweeping second hand of the clock behind Dr. Menon's head, the relentless pushing, sliding, straining pressure inside me, between my legs.

Suddenly, the intensity popped, and I felt the baby's body, distinctly, sliding through me.

"The head is out. Pant without pushing just for a moment." Dr. Menon and the nurse busied themselves with a blue bulbed syringe, clearing the baby's mouth and throat. Claude started to cry. "I can see our baby's face," he said.

I could no longer contain the pressure building inside me. In a single rush, the rest of his body slid into the world.

"It's a boy! It's a boy!" Claude exclaimed, tears sliding down his cheeks. The two of us couldn't take our eyes off our son's slippery form. Everyone, even the busiest nurse, was smiling. Although Will's umbilical cord was still attached to the unborn placenta inside my body, Dr. Menon laid him, cheek to breast, against my chest. As I held our son in my arms, he gazed at me quietly, not crying, awake. Claude leaned over and kissed the top of Will's head, then turned to me. The two of us looked into each other, transparent and trembling as if we were each seeing the other for the first time.

Unraveled

Dr. Menon quietly interrupted our reverie by handing Claude a pair of scissors, instructing him where to make the cut in the umbilical cord. I stroked the top of Will's head and brushed my lips across his cheek. Instinctively, his head turned toward my breast. I slipped my nipple between his lips and he began to suck. I felt a searing goodness being pulled from inside me. As he nursed, Will's blue, deep-seeing eyes never left mine. For a single, timeless moment, the rest of the world vanished, and everything was my son and me.

INHERITANCE

CLAUDE AND I, *giddy with happiness, we're bringing our little boy home. As we wound through the quiet streets of our neighborhood, I stared out the window and could not believe how much had changed in the two days since Will's birth. Everything familiar looked different and somehow more beautiful, as if the light falling on it had passed through a special filter, allowing it to be seen more perfectly and precisely than before.*

Glancing at Claude's profile, I was filled with a sense that everything we had done together since we'd married five years before had been in preparation for this. Each decision we had made, from finishing college to sending Claude to graduate school, and saving enough money to buy our first home in a town with excellent schools, forty-five minutes from Claude's parents, had been part of a carefully orchestrated plan. Although we had married young, when I was twenty and Claude was twenty-five, each of us was sure that, like our parents, we'd be married forever, and the two of us shared a sober determination to make an even better life for our children than the lives we'd lived so far.

Feeling my eyes on him, Claude turned. "I love you," I said, blowing him a kiss. He smiled as we pulled into the drive. Climbing out of the car, I gathered the diaper bag and small suitcase. Claude opened the door behind me, unhooked the safety latch, and lifted Will in his infant carrier from the backseat. I followed the two of them as they passed through the gate of the white picket fence. The stone path leading to the back door led us past the rose garden. In early December, the bushes were mostly a tumble of bare branches, but the manicured lawn of the backyard was still a deep green. As we approached the back door of our little Cape Cod, Claude suddenly stopped and turned. Tipping Will's infant seat slightly forward, he said, solemnly but with a sparkle in his eye, "Someday son, this will all be yours."

The two of us had grinned at each other, drunk in our shared love for our son. Looking back, I realize that neither of us had any way of knowing, then, how far from reality our shared dreams were.

UNCHARTED WATERS

WILL HAD ALREADY CRAWLED *halfway up the steps when he turned, plopping his diapered bottom on the stair behind him, and giggled at me. Standing two steps below him, I smiled and clapped my hands encouragingly. I was trying to hide my concern, not wanting to scare him, half wondering if I should whisk him up and away from danger, but too excited to interrupt his climb. I couldn't wait to see the look on his face when he finally reached the top.*

Will turned back to the task, and I slowly followed. As soon as he reached the top step, he scooted his chubby legs around until he was in a sitting position and, beaming at me, began clapping his hands. His delight in this new perspective, looking down on me, was worth every breathless moment I had experienced during his climb. I grinned and clapped too, reaching over to kiss his cheek.

"Good job, Will! You did it," I said, feeling that I couldn't have been more proud if he had just scaled Mt. Everest. "You

must be so proud of yourself," I said, reaching down to pick him up.

Two hours later, my friend Ann and I were sitting in her living room, which was comfortably cluttered with toys, unfolded laundry, and half-drunk cups of coffee. Will and Ann's daughter Jillian were crawling around the gated childproofed space. I admired Ann. She was the kind of woman I secretly wanted to be. She was smart and sexy, and seemed sure of herself in a way that I wasn't. She was finishing her graduate degree in child psychology and was unapologetically in love with Mark, her second husband, a talented and successful graphic artist and the father of Jillian.

Ann seemed to know everything when it came to the health and safety of her child. I was sure she had memorized every dot and mole on Jillian's body, while I hadn't even remembered to count Will's fingers and toes in the moments after his birth. Ann seemed unconcerned about what other people might think about the way her house or life looked; as long as Jillian was happy, everything was okay. I was pretty sure my priorities weren't as noble or clear. I knew I loved Will as much as Ann loved Jillian, but I still considered the care and running of my home one of my primary responsibilities. It really mattered to me, the way things looked.

Every morning, after Claude left for work and Will went down for his morning nap, I scurried around, emptying and

*loading the dishwasher, dusting, vacuuming, making the beds
and straightening each room. I had a list of daily, weekly, and
monthly household tasks taped to the refrigerator door, as well
as a frequently updated grocery list, organized according to the
supermarket aisles. I prided myself on my efficiency and orga-
nization, and loved it when Claude raved to friends and family about how quickly I had bounced back after Will's birth.
Everything I did was done with one eye open to the way it
would look to someone else.*

*Now, listening to Ann, I watched Will practice pulling
himself up to stand while Jillian crawled around on the living
room floor. Ann suddenly paused in the middle of a sentence
when she saw what Will was doing.*

*"Oh, my God! Look at him," she exclaimed. "He's going
to be walking before you know it!"*

*I smiled, trying to look more modest than I felt. "You
won't believe what he did this morning," I said, and then re-
counted how he had crawled up the steps to the second floor.
When I finished, I knew I was beaming, but I couldn't help
it; I felt as proud as I had the moment he'd reached the top.
Ann, however, was more horrified than impressed.*

*"No! Where were you? Don't tell me you were there and
let him do it. Now you're going to have to watch him like a
hawk to keep him from doing it again," Ann said.*

*My smile slid off my flushed cheeks as I took a sip of my
tea to camouflage my embarrassment. Of course Ann was*

right! What had possessed me to allow Will to do something so foolish and unsafe? Closing my eyes briefly, I vowed to be more attentive to my child's health and well-being. No matter how clean or well organized my house was, it couldn't make up for the shame I now felt as a mother.

NO FOOLING

I BENT DOWN, placed my hands on either side of Will's face, and kissed both of his cheeks. "Remember, Muffin, Mommy always comes back," I said.

"Yes, Momma, I know," he replied, throwing his arms around me for a final, quick hug before running to join the other two-year-olds in his day care class.

For the past year and a half, since Will was three months old, I had been working part-time as a financial analyst for a large telecommunications company. There had never been any question between Claude and me that I would return to my job after taking a maternity leave. We both knew that I was a different kind of mother—more capable and independent—than our mothers had been when we were growing up. Besides the fact that we could certainly use the additional income, it was important to me that Will and any other children we might have understand that though I was a wife and mother, I was also a woman who had individual interests and a successful career.

Unraveled

But lately, the last thing I wanted to do each morning was pull on another pair of panty hose, leave Will in the arms of someone else, and pretend to care about a corporate job. Becoming a mother had rearranged my priorities in a way I hadn't expected. I couldn't tell if it was because I was unusually efficient or shamefully unmotivated that I now seemed to spend most of my time shuffling papers around on my desk, leaving file drawers haphazardly open, and making sure there was a complicated-looking spreadsheet on the screen of my computer in case a manager popped into my office unannounced. Stretching ten hours of work into a twenty-hour week seemed more exhausting than the actual work was.

Now, as I weaved in and out of highway traffic on my way to work, I didn't feel as certain about what I wanted as I had just a few months before. Rather than tailored suits and business meetings, a part of me longed for turtleneck sweaters and jeans and play dates with other moms and kids. It wasn't that I had lost interest in being an independent woman, or that I didn't value the idea of a career; it was simply that I couldn't help wondering if it might be possible to find a sense of meaning and usefulness in my life that wasn't connected to the amount of money I made or the work I did.

MONDAY

MY EYES WERE STILL CLOSED as I lay in bed, in-haling the cool morning breeze, feeling the weight of the quilt pulled up to my chin. I extended my arms and legs across the full length and width of the bed, savoring the spaciousness, knowing I could stay there as long as I wanted. Too excited, though, to lie still for long, I finally opened my eyes and sat up, swinging my legs over the side of the bed. Through the curtains in the window, I could see fields of grass, stretching across rolling hills to the faraway edges of trees.

I stood up. The silence in the room was as palpable as it had been the night before, but the light of morning had softened its effect on me. As I slipped on my robe and collected my toiletries and towel, I moved slowly so as not to disturb its spell. Everything seemed tinged with a kind of magic. Even the soap I had brought from home smelled sweeter than I remembered as I showered in the tiny bathroom across the hall.

Drying my body quickly, I pulled on a long cotton skirt and T-shirt, and made my way barefoot down to the kitchen and dining room, one floor below. The night before, Mary had showed me where to find freshly sliced bread, granola, yogurt, and bowls of fruit. While the coffee brewed, I slathered two pieces of toast with homemade jam and peanut butter. Carefully balancing the tray with my breakfast on it, I climbed three flights of stairs to the top floor of the barn.

There, in a book-lined nook, I sat in a rocking chair, in front of a triangular window, overlooking miles of fields, hills, and trees. Sipping my coffee and nibbling toast while I rocked, I felt my body filling with a sense of exhilaration as I realized the whole day stretched before me, unscheduled. I could do anything I wanted, with no responsibility to anyone's needs but my own. My life, like the sun in my eyes, was rising into a brand new sky.

A TINY LADYBUG made her way across the page of my opened journal. Watching her slow, patient progress across what I imagined for her was an unfamiliar expanse of white, I appreciated the simplicity of her journey— just a shell, some wings, and a bit of determination. By comparison, my journey and my children's, which had started in New Jersey three days before, had required the kind of advance planning, packing, and logistical consideration of a large-scale, military operation.

On the day we left, I had risen before dawn and loaded the minivan with suitcases, coolers of drinks and snacks, and several backpacks full of books and toys. It was a two-day journey from our home in New Jersey to where Will, Margaret, and Madelaine would be staying with my sister and her family in Michigan, but we had packed enough supplies, games, and activities to last us for four. After waking the children, I had fed them breakfast, helped them get dressed, and then made sure each of them went to the bathroom before they climbed into the car. Claude had come downstairs to see us off, embracing each of the children but barely looking at me. As I backed the minivan out of the drive, all three kids had waved to their dad and then shouted "Ya-hoo!" in unison. The four of us could have been headed west in a covered wagon for all the excitement we felt.

Now, rolling over onto my back, I felt the matted comfort of the old quilt under my bare legs, and the soft cotton of the white eyelet pillowcase under my head. Lying in the cool shade, I caught glimpses of the afternoon sun as it danced between the spreading branches of the maple tree above. The color of the ladybug's shell, the whisper of the maple leaves tossing in the breeze, the scent of crushed grass beneath my quilt—as I inhaled the sounds, colors, and scents of life around me, part of me wished that my children were here to share the beauty and simplicity of this moment.

Yet I also knew that it was only in being alone that I would be able to do what I came here to do, to have any hope of remembering everything I had almost forgotten.

IT WAS LATE AFTERNOON, and I was pacing around my room, feeling unhinged and restless. The residue of warmth and peace from my time under the maple tree had been tossed aside. My brow was wrinkled and my heart pounded inexplicably in my chest. I was out of breath but not tired, rested but not at peace. I couldn't help wondering if I had made a mistake in coming. After all, a voice was whispering in my heart, what kind of mother would so willingly be separated from her young children for ten days?

I also could not shake the feeling that something was coming, that I was here to meet someone. It was entirely possible, I reasoned, that my sense of loneliness and the pain of separation from my kids was causing me to wish for someone else to talk to, to reassure me. Either that, or I was going slightly crazy in the unfamiliar solitude and silence.

I heard a phone ringing in the office downstairs. I

raced to answer it, but the door to the office was locked. While I tried to figure out if there was a way to open it, the phone stopped ringing. Standing outside the door, I began to panic. What if it had been Claude trying to call me, or my sister Laura, or one of my kids? Although I knew they all had the phone number to my cell phone in case of an emergency, it didn't matter. The fear I was feeling now wasn't rational; it oozed like lava out of some dark place in my heart.

Plodding slowly up the stairs to my room, I began to cry. I felt helpless, impotent, disconnected from everything I had known as my life: my house, my family, and my routine. Part of me felt frightened by the idea that Claude and my children could go on with their day-to-day lives without me. I missed my kids and longed to feel their arms wrapped around my neck, inhale the scent of their sweetness, listen to their voices telling me about their day. I felt guilty, physically sick inside, for having felt excited about being able to come here on my own, for choosing to spend time away from them.

Throwing myself on my bed, loud, hiccupping sobs began to pour out of my chest. My heart felt waterlogged with loneliness. I wanted now, more than anything, to be able to take my children into my arms and apologize to them for every angry, frustrated word I had ever uttered as a mother. I knew that my family deserved to know the happier, grateful, joyful woman I had been in the shade of the tree, hours before, rather than the wife and mother I had been lately, who was more a tight, angry expression of my frustrations and fears.

Finally, exhausted from crying, I sat up in bed, wiped my nose with a tissue, and blotted tears from my cheeks. My eyes fell on the kneeling bench, along the wall, beneath the second window. I stood up and walked over to it, then slowly lowered my knees until they rested on the padded edge. Bowing my head, I closed my eyes, and breathed. Gradually, I felt my heart begin to beat more slowly, as I allowed myself to rest.

I realized then that even though my children and I were not in the same place, in some important way we shared the same heart. And my responsibility to them, to my family, was to use this time away to grow ever more appreciative and stronger. Then, and only then, I would be a better mother for having gone away.

Maria Housden

HEART ON A LIMB

CLAUDE AND I *were holding hands, our bare feet making side-by-side tracks in the white sand. Will, his bare bottom already tanned from days in the Florida sun, ran ahead, chasing sandpipers fanning across the beach in waves. Weeks before, when Claude had asked me where I wanted to go on vacation, I had said, "California" as I always did. We had both laughed when he replied, "No, I've already been there. Let's go somewhere else," because that was what he always said.*

After having endured the shared pain and disappointment of two miscarriages in the past year, all the ways we were predictable together felt like a tremendous relief. It was also true that another baby was now alive and growing in me. This pregnancy, three and a half months along, seemed to have passed the critical point. I was finally coming closer to being the mother I had always wanted to be, now that we were making the leap from one child to two.

As Claude and I walked along, following Will, I savored

32

the feeling of my smaller hand in Claude's larger one. It was comforting to feel his presence, his strength beside me. Inhaling the salty air, I was aware of a deep sense of contentment rising in my bones, and I prayed that Claude was feeling it too. Losing the two pregnancies had catapulted us into a kind of isolated aloneness as each of us tried to cope with our disappointment and grief, and at the same time we had been brought closer together, feeling more determined than ever to create the larger family we both wanted.

Ahead of us, Will stopped short, turned, and began running full speed toward Claude and me with arms outstretched. "Mommy," he said, wrapping his arms around my legs, "I want to give our new baby a kiss."

Claude and I smiled at each other as I bent down on one knee and lifted my shirt. Will leaned over, ran his small hands over the top of my bulging belly, and gently gave it a kiss. As Will stood up, Claude reached down and swung him up into his arms, planting a kiss on his head.

"Hey, buddy, do you want a baby brother or a baby sister?" he asked.

"Oh, Daddy," Will replied, "I want a big brother, bigger than me!"

POETRY

*I STUMBLED INTO HANNAH'S ROOM, barely able
to open my eyes as I made my way in the dark. My full,
aching breasts had begun leaking down the front of my night-
gown at the sound of her first cry. The light of the moon fil-
tered softly through the blinds as I lifted Hannah out of the crib
and settled into the rocking chair. Leaning my head back, I
closed my eyes as she began to nurse. I felt a part of myself
sinking into the dark behind my lids and lowered into a deep
pool, while the rest of my body, although exhausted, stayed
awake, aware of the soft weight of Hannah's diapered bottom
in the palm of my hand.*

*I lost track of time and place as the two of us drifted there.
Just as when she was inside my body only months ago, it
seemed as if there was no distinction between us. The only
movement was my rocking and the back-and-forth sucking of
Hannah's lips, the only sensation the tingly drawing down
of the milk from deep inside my breast.*

Unraveled

Eventually, Hannah's sucking began to slow and, not wanting her to fall fully asleep before finishing, I raised my head from the back of the chair and slipped a finger between her lips and my swollen nipple to break the suction. As I lifted her away from my breast, a few drops of milk spilled warm from her mouth onto my skin. I lightly kissed the top of her forehead, one, two, three times, and then laid her against my body again, guiding her mouth to my other nipple before she had a chance to protest. I smiled as her tiny fist closed around one of my fingers and she nuzzled closer and began to nurse.

As I gazed at her in the moonlight, at her long lashes lying against the translucent skin on her cheek, I felt myself drawn into a softer, more primal awareness of the night. This silence, I knew, was the secret source of every mother's strength, a place where the quietest work of the universe happens, while the rest of the world sleeps.

SHOWDOWN WITH ROBIN HOOD

IT WAS A SHOWDOWN between Robin Hood from the Dark Side and me, his mother. Will, now four years old, stood defiantly, one hand on his hip, wearing a pair of green tights, a green felt cape, and a red cowboy hat. A plastic bow hung like a necklace around his neck. In his other fist he was gripping an arrow, jabbing it in my direction.

"Grrrrrrr . . ." he growled, his face scrunched into a fierce grimace, teeth clenched together.

Three feet away, I stayed where I was. Crazy with fury, I had passed angry long ago. If he moved any closer, I thought I might grab him, whack his bottom, and stuff him into a closet. I'd have done anything to make him stop. Two hours before, I had been congratulating myself for having orchestrated a perfect day; I couldn't believe how fast my fortune had changed.

Earlier that morning, I had woken before anyone else, washed my hair, put on makeup, and packed the diaper bag.

When the kids and Claude woke, I had unloaded the dishwasher and packed Claude's lunch, then spoon-fed Hannah in her high chair while Claude and Will ate breakfast. Later, after Claude left for work, I had dressed Hannah in new pink overalls and said a brief prayer of thanks when Will, without argument, agreed to wear a clean pair of jeans and a shirt that matched.

Well rested and organized, with two perfectly groomed children in tow, I had arrived at Friday-morning play group promptly at 10 A.M. Sitting at my friend Karen's kitchen table, sipping coffee with the other mothers, I had breathed a quiet sigh of relief. Although being a mother felt the most natural thing to me, whenever I compared myself to others, I felt an odd sort of anxiety that I wasn't doing it the way it was supposed to be done. I would regularly listen without comment while friends obsessed over their children's diets—whether foods were organic or contained too much sugar—too embarrassed to admit that I had, more than once, opened a bag of Oreos at 9 in the morning simply to keep Will quiet in the car.

That wasn't the only secret I was harboring.

Something was happening with Will. In the past few months he had begun talking back and openly defying me, sometimes poking and pushing other kids. It was as if he were overdosing on testosterone. I had patience with him at first— my parents had spanked me when I was a child, and I had vowed long ago not to revisit the same sin on my children; I was on a mission to create perfect children by being the perfectly loving, nonviolent mother.

But as the days and weeks wore on, Will's behavior hadn't changed. In fact, it seemed to get worse. And so did I. I had started yelling, which appeared, at first glance, to shock him into listening. But then he got used to it and began to ignore me again. I had tried putting him in time-outs next, but when he refused to stay in one place, I would get angrier, grab him, and roughly sit him on the edge of the bed. Finally, I began spanking him—not hard or often, but enough to feel ashamed and sorry later. I had made plenty of tearful apologies to him afterward, which only seemed to confuse him more. But I was at a loss for what to do, and it seemed that whenever I got aggressive and angry, Will's defiant, aggressive behavior stopped. I desperately wanted to believe that Will's difficulties were temporary—a problem that I could nip in the bud before anyone else noticed.

I should have known better.

Thirty minutes into play group, even before my second cup of coffee had cooled, a piercing wail rose from the playroom. Seven mothers, including me, shot out of their chairs. Even with Hannah in my arms, I managed to be one of the first on the scene. It wasn't pretty. As the other mothers and I burst into the room, Will, a plastic knight's breastplate strapped to his chest, was standing over a bawling Eric, waving his arms triumphantly over his head.

Will turned to me. "*Eric was being mean to us!*" he cried as I glared at him, trying to assess the damage.

I helped Eric to his feet and kneeled in front of Will, my back to the others so they couldn't see my face.

"Tell Eric you're sorry," I said to Will through clenched teeth. Eric wiped his nose with the sleeve of his shirt, while the other three- and four-year-olds stood to one side, solemnly watching what was happening.

"No. He was the one being mean!" Will retorted, stomping his foot on the floor. "Eric should say 'sorry' to me."

Just then, Hannah, who had been asleep in my arms, woke up and began screaming. Eric started crying again and ran to his mother. I felt the other women's eyes on me, imagining them, accusing and smug, outraged on behalf of their innocent ones. It was, I realized, a situation that could not be easily remedied. I decided to cut my losses. I handed Hannah to Karen, picked Will up, and carried him, kicking and thrashing, out to the car. Both kids screamed all the way home. I glared at Will in the rearview mirror. I felt outraged for having had to abandon one of the few opportunities I had to spend time with people who didn't need me to help them to the potty. More than anything, though, I was furious with him for "outing" me as the bad mother I was.

Now, an hour and a half later, the two of us were facing off again. Will was refusing to change out of his Robin Hood costume before going to the grocery store. As I stood there, I *couldn't help wondering what had happened to the sweet little boy whose slippery form had slid out of my body three and a half years earlier, the baby who had slept on my chest every day in the warmth of the afternoon sun. I had, obviously, in a little less than four years, managed to ruin the perfect little being who had been entrusted to me. I suddenly felt completely exhausted and my anger at Will vanished. Overwhelmed by my complete and utter failure as a mother, I sat down on the floor and began to cry.*

As I wept helplessly, my face buried in my arm, I heard Will's footsteps approaching and then felt his arm slide around my neck.

"What's the matter, Mommy?" he asked, bending down to peek at me.

I lifted my head, wiping the tears from my cheeks.

"I'm sorry, Will." I said. "I just don't feel like a very good mommy right now."

"Why?" he said, adjusting his cape to keep it from slipping over his shoulder. "Is it because I want to be Robin Hood at the grocery store?"

In that moment, I saw something I had never seen in the same way before. As Will stood there, looking at me, waiting for my answer, I realized that he was a completely unique, intact human being in a little person's body entirely separate from me. Yes, he was dressed like a bad movie version of Robin Hood, but what did that matter? I was dressed as a bad soap opera's version of a suburban housewife. Together, we made quite a pair.

I began to laugh and pulled Will into my arms. I understood then that I had been pouring so much energy into trying to make us and our lives look the way I thought they were supposed to look that I was missing all the wonderful, unique things we already were. Just because I would never consider going to the grocery store dressed as Robin Hood didn't mean that Will couldn't. In fact, it was inevitable that there would be many, many more things that Will was going to like to do, to eat, to try, to be that I would have no interest in. His preferences for this or that had little or nothing to do with me.

And as for my frustrations with his behavior earlier in the day, of course Will was going to have difficulties learning to get along with other kids, managing his angry feelings, deciding what he liked and what he didn't—I was still, at age twenty-nine, struggling with the same things. But the important distinction I hadn't been able to make until this moment was that I was not Will's difficulty. My responsibility as a mother was to have compassion for Will, while at the same time trying my best to teach him how to deal with his feelings and the situations he might find himself in. His behavior, good or bad, belonged to him; what I did in response to his behavior belonged to me.

Our differences and difficulties weren't personal to each other; they were simply part of who we were. And the truest way I could express my love for Will would be to respect and celebrate both our connection as mother and son and our separateness as two, unique human beings.

"Come on, Will," I said, holding his hand as I got to my feet. "Let's go to the grocery store dressed exactly as we are. After all, even Robin Hood has to eat!"

FIRST STEPS

THE MID-JULY SUN *was hot on our faces and shoulders, but the water along the stretch of isolated beach on Lake Superior where we were walking had risen from the icy depths of the deepest of the Great Lakes, so our bare feet were red with cold. Hannah, ten months old, was asleep in the infant carrier strapped to Claude's back, a yellow pacifier in her mouth and a ruffled white sun hat on her head. She had spent much of the morning pushing her stroller around our campsite, Claude and I cheering her on and congratulating each other that, like Will, she was going to be an early walker. I knew that anyone watching us would see from the way we were together that we were the perfect family, especially if they knew we also had a handsome young son.*

My parents had invited Will to spend a week with them at the Cherry Festival in Traverse City, so Claude and I had decided to continue north with Hannah after dropping Will off, and spend the week camping and hiking along the National

Lakeshore. It felt great to have stepped away from the busyness of our daily lives. Now that we had become used to juggling the needs of two children, it felt positively easy to take care of just one. We had pitched our tent on the sand, under a stand of pines, almost a week before. And although we had begun to feel more and more relaxed as the week progressed, the decision we had to make still hung in the air between us.

Claude and I were at a crossroads in our life. For too long, now, Claude had felt unhappy at work. The most progressive and experimental cellular technologies were being developed in companies on the east and west coasts, which meant, as a design engineer, if Claude wanted to work with the best, we would to have to move. But to me, the thought of uprooting our family at this time in our lives didn't feel like such a good idea. In the past year we had experienced a number of significant changes. I had quit my part-time job as a financial analyst soon after Hannah's birth, and although it was a dream Claude and I both shared that he would provide financially for our growing family so that I could be with our children at home, it seemed that neither of us felt happier or less frustrated, despite our new arrangement. The arguments between us had been growing louder and more hurtful, and more than once I had allowed myself to flirt with the idea of a divorce.

I couldn't help thinking of a story about Picasso I had recently heard. After sitting in front of Gertrude Stein for more than three months, painting her portrait, one day Picasso had

44

stood up and asked her to leave. "I can't see you anymore when I look," he had said. For a long time now, I had felt as if I were experiencing the same thing. After eight and a half years of marriage, it was unsettling that I felt more and more distant from Claude, rather than closer. Our love for our children was one thing we unquestionably shared, but no matter how much that meant to me, it did not feel like enough. The life we had constellated together was feeling more like an idea than a reality, much less familiar and comfortable than either of us had expected. I had been afraid that a move might leave us both feeling even more vulnerable, and further compromise the already frayed connection between us.

Now, though, watching Claude pick his way along the path ahead of me, moving carefully so as not to wake Hannah, the contrast between the sullen, frustrated man who left the house each morning to go to a job he did not love and the sun-tanned, smiling man ahead felt too great for me to ignore. This man, I realized, was the adventuresome, curious man I had fallen in love with. Perhaps Claude was right, that a change of life and change of scenery was exactly what we needed. And as his wife, it was up to me to support and encourage him to make the best, right decision for our family.

Running ahead to catch up, I grabbed Claude's hand and smiled at him when he turned. "I think we should go for it," I said. "Your career is important, and you deserve to feel good about what you do. Besides, no matter where we move, with our kids and each other, we'll be able to make any house a home."

Claude's wide grin was the only response I needed. Throwing our arms around each other, I realized that Hannah wasn't the only one taking her first steps. I felt happy to have made such an important decision, with Claude's interests at heart, and I couldn't help hoping, having made it, that I was finally on my way to being the wife I had always wanted to be, the wife Claude had always wanted to have.

SHADES OF GRAY

I WAITED in the silence of the examining room, listening to the sound of Claude's footsteps pacing outside the door. I breathed deeply, trying to collect my thoughts and steel myself for what might be next. Despite the anxiety I was feeling, I felt grateful to have been able at least to think clearly enough to ask Claude not to come in. The terrified look in his red-rimmed eyes would make it difficult for anyone to believe the story I had decided to tell.

My thoughts were interrupted by a knock on the door.

"Come in," I said, as confidently as my voice would allow. The door opened and a white-coated doctor entered. I felt surprised and relieved to see that she was a woman, and then a flash of panic as I wondered if a woman might sense my fear more easily than a man.

"Hello, I'm Dr. Martha Gray," she said, advancing toward me, tucking her clipboard under her arm while extending her other hand. I felt my sense of panic rising as I became aware

that my hands were shaking, and my heart was thumping in my chest. Dr. Gray's expression, however, didn't change. She shook my hand and then glanced briefly at the words the nurse in the triage area had written on a piece of paper that was now fastened beneath the board's clip.

"It says here that you sustained some sort of injury and now have blood in your urine." She looked up from the clipboard, directly into my eyes. "I need you to tell me exactly what happened."

My ears felt plugged, filled with the sound of the blood that was rushing into my head. The doctor's gaze was steady on me as I blinked twice, swallowed, and then took a deep, shaking breath.

"I fell. I slipped and fell on the concrete steps outside our back door." My voice sounded fine, stronger than I expected it to. I cleared my throat again and continued more confidently. "It was icy," I explained. "I caught the corner of the step as I fell, on the left side. I think the corner of the step bruised my left kidney."

Dr. Gray continued to look at me quietly. I opened my mouth to say more and then closed it. I couldn't tell from the look in her eyes whether she had believed me. The doctor reached for her stethoscope. I willed my heartbeat to slow. I took a deep, shuddering breath. Dr. Gray listened for a moment to my chest, and then gently raised my sweater to look at the left side of my back. I felt my life energy floating in and out *of my body as I struggled to stay calm and tried to erase the images in my head of what had happened in our family room less than an hour ago.*

Already, it seemed as if it were only a dream. I couldn't even remember what we had been arguing about. What I did remember was Claude ignoring me, his eyes staring straight ahead at the television, his lips pressed together, refusing to acknowledge me. I was yelling, begging him to answer me. Both of us had forgotten that Hannah was witnessing all of it, sitting on the carpeted steps, halfway up the stairs.

Staring at the linoleum tiles on the examining room floor, I saw the image of me screaming into Claude's face, and him rising up from the couch, arms bent at the elbows, flailing. Somehow, his left elbow had slammed into the lower left side of my back. I could remember falling hard on the carpeted floor, and on my way down, seeing Hannah watching me fall.

I had lain there for the longest moment. Then, his hand shaking, Claude had helped me up, and the two of us had stood, facing each other, stunned. I had turned away from Claude without speaking and started up the stairs. Picking Hannah up, I had carried her to her room and sat in the rocking chair with her, rocking and crying softly, apologizing over and over to her. Hannah, unusually quiet, had eventually fallen asleep. I had then put her in her crib and gone to the bathroom.

It was then I realized that my urine was pink. I had gone

downstairs to tell Claude, who was sitting on the couch in the dark.

"There's blood in my urine," I told him, woodenly. "I think I should go to the emergency room."

Looking now into the doctor's doubting eyes, I held her gaze. I knew that the man outside this room was not capable of the things these people might want to accuse him of. Telling the truth about what had happened could only do more damage than good. Undoubtedly, our heightened emotions, good and bad, were due to the fact that, in a little more than a week, we were scheduled to move to our new home in New Jersey.

More than anything, though, I was certain that what had happened was not one person's fault or the other's. It was a warning to Claude and me that the problems between us were more serious than we had understood. And far from wanting to run from them, I had seen today, in Claude's concerned, frightened eyes, a man I could love, a thoughtful man capable of caring for me.

Unraveled

TUESDAY

I HELD THE BURNING MATCH carefully between my fingertips, and lit the three white votive candles on the altar. Sitting on one of the straight-backed chairs arranged in a semicircle in the barn's small chapel, I stared at the large wooden cross hanging from the ceiling and watched the sun rise through the stained glass window. The room was silent except for the occasional sputter of a candle flame and muffled footfalls from the floor above. Already, my third day here, I felt closer to God, not only as an idea, but as a presence, a source of guidance that knew, even if I didn't, who I was and what I needed to do.

I was no longer alone in the barn. The night before, while Mary, Gene, and I savored a dinner of homemade bread and warm stew, the sound of tires on the gravel drive had interrupted the silence. The elderly couple had risen without speaking and gone outside to greet the visitor. I had heard the soft hum of voices, the opening and closing of a door, and footsteps on the stairs. Mary told me later, while the two of us washed the dinner dishes, that she had settled the new arrival, a writer, in a room on the barn's top floor. The four of us would be eating lunches and dinners together in the dining room, and the silence at meals would continue to be observed.

At the time, I hadn't felt even the mildest sense of curiosity about who this other was. Now though, listening to the sounds from above, knowing that they were the footfalls of a writer, I began to wonder. I had always imagined myself a writer, ever since I was twelve. But I had imagined myself many other things too, a pioneer woman, a painter, a world traveler, and I hadn't become any of those things either.

Watching the flames of the candles dance in the bursts of breeze coming in from an open window, I realized that all of those things, like the retreat I had once only imagined, were possibilities that only needed a breath of attention in order to come alive again in me. And if that were true, the first thing I wanted was for the presence of this writer to inspire me to return to the book about Hannah's life and death that I'd started and stopped writing two years before.

Unraveled

A LIGHT, MISTY RAIN was falling, damping down the dusty road as I walked toward the mailbox, carrying a stack of postcards I had written to Claude, my sister, and my kids. Although I was still missing Will, Margaret, and Madelaine terribly, it was comforting to know that the three of them were together. I had grown up loving the fact that I had two younger sisters and a younger brother, and I knew from my own experience what good company and how much fun siblings could be.

Despite the rain, dragonflies and bees continued to flit and buzz between flowers along the road, and ahead in the distance, streaks of sun pierced through patches of gray cloud. My hair was pulled back, caught in a large barrette, and covered by a wide-brimmed straw hat. I was wearing a long, cotton skirt and leather boots. Holding my head high, I was aware of the length of my stride and the swing of my arms. Smiling, I realized this was how I used to feel when I wandered around our neighborhood, wrapped in sheets, pretending to be a pioneer woman as a young girl.

Already, after only two nights on my own, I could feel my body unlearning its usual routine, reorienting itself to the track of the sun across the sky, to the rhythm and heat of the summer days. Reaching down, I slid a long blade of grass with its heavily seeded head from the stem of its root, rolled it between my finger and thumb, and

inhaled its sweet scent. I felt a heightened sense of awareness, a deeper, more natural relationship with everything
around me. Here, although I felt as far from my other life
as I could possibly be, I felt closer than ever to the
woman I'd always been.

Walking down the road, I glanced at the words on the
postcards I'd written to my kids and smiled when I imagined how glad they'd be to receive mail from me. Although I almost didn't want to admit it, even to myself, I
didn't feel the same way about Claude. I had written to
him more from a sense of obligation than of joy. My
sense of family, I realized now, was the image of me with
my kids. And even though Claude was my husband, my
primary interest in my relationship with him was his role
as my children's father.

I stared ahead of me, into the expanse of the sky's
gray, and tried to remember if I had always felt this way.
Though there had certainly been times in our marriage
when I could remember loving Claude as a man, and not
specifically as a father, lately it seemed our marriage was
more a project we were working on than anything about
love. For many years, Claude had been telling me he was
unhappy with me and our marriage, and in response I
had tried to become the woman and wife Claude wanted
rather than the woman I was.

I knew, too, that I could not blame only Claude for

how far I had drifted from my sense of what was possible for me. I had believed, as much as he had, that to be a good wife, I was supposed to change who I was and, at the same time, be even more accepting of him. Now, though, I knew that I had to give myself the same permission to be imperfect that I had given Claude, and if being more of who I was meant that Claude would like me less, it was a chance I was now willing to take. It was entirely possible that Claude and I were two boats that, once tied together, had now drifted far enough apart in the turning tide to see that the cord connecting one to the other had been severed long ago.

Reaching the end of the lane, where the dirt road met asphalt, I opened the mailbox and kissed each postcard before leaning it against the others inside. The last, Claude's, I held for a moment longer, wondering where my words would find him, and if, in reading them, he would sense the release of my grip.

HALFWAY THROUGH MY LUNCH, I was watching the chickadees outside the window. After my walk to the mailbox and a late-morning nap in my room, I was filled with a palpable sense of connection with everything in my life, including the tiny birds I was watching, pecking at their seed, the sound of another's chair scraping across the wood floor, and the slightly bitter taste of arugula in my mouth. I didn't even glance up when the person across from me sat down. His place, where Mary and Gene had set it, was directly across the table from mine. When I finally looked over at him, it was his clear-seeing blue eyes I saw first.

He was a strong-looking man, about fifty years old, with a kind, laugh-lined face, large, long-fingered hands, and silver-gray hair cropped short. He was smiling at me in a familiar way, as if he were surprised to see me. My heart was a mirrored pool as we gazed into each other without words, filled with a sense of joy and delight. And although I had never seen his face or his form before, in that single, timeless moment I felt as if I knew the heart of this man and recognized both my separateness and my connection to him. I knew, too, there was no need to try to do or say anything in response; he and I were the reason we were here, and whatever needed to happen between us, it was all already done.

I PROPPED THE DOOR to my room open with a large fieldstone and sat in the armchair, breathing deeply, my heart thumping wildly in my chest. Even though the two of us, respecting the retreat center's rule about silence at mealtimes, hadn't yet exchanged a single word, I was hoping he would come. Picking up and putting my book down too many times to count, my mind felt empty and yet too fully engaged to read. Finally, I heard footsteps descending the stairs, then coming louder and closer, rounding the corner. My body was thrumming with aliveness, my eyes looking for his when he got to the door of my room and stopped.

Seeing him, I instantly felt more sober than excited. The moment felt weighted with importance, and from the look on his face, he felt the same way. Neither of us smiled as I gestured to him to come in. As he crossed over the threshold, I chose to remain seated, and studied him while his eyes scanned the room. He was wearing a white linen shirt, blue linen trousers, and brown leather clogs. The part of me that was already writing a story between us was relieved to see that he was tall, almost the same height as me. He briefly sat on the edge of my bed, then changed his mind, and stood.

"My name is Roger Housden," he said finally. I caught my breath at the sound of his voice, momentarily discombobulated to hear his accent. "I'm English," he continued, "a writer. Two weeks ago, I sold almost everything I had, moved out of the home I shared with a woman I loved and lived with for thirteen years, and came to America. I was invited by a nonprofit foundation to spend a week at this retreat center, finishing my next book. Writing, I find, is solitary work. Because of that, and because I've just broken off with a woman I love, I intend to spend this period of time on my own, thinking about what is next in my life. The last thing I'm looking for is to be involved in another relationship."

I nodded, my mind trying to take in everything he had said without getting distracted by the conversations parts of myself were already having inside my head. From the first moment, I had known this man was nothing like anyone I had ever known. But now, with only a little more information, the quietest part of me wanted to know more, while another felt so intimidated by our obvious differences, it wanted out.

"I'm Maria Martell," I said, setting my insecurities aside and extending my hand. The strength and warmth of his grasp calmed me further. I gathered my courage and barreled on. "I was raised in Michigan, but now I and my family are living in New Jersey. I'm married. My husband, Claude, and I have been married for fifteen and a half years. I've had four children," I gestured toward the window where my photographs were hung. "My daughter Hannah died of cancer four years ago at the age of three," I paused, wanting to get this next part right. "Although my marriage has been going through a rocky time, and I'm not sure yet what is going to happen, I do believe that Claude and I are each other's best option.

And if things don't work out between us, there is no way I want to get involved for quite some time with anyone else."

I stopped, surprised and amazed that I had been able to be so concise and honest. Roger smiled. "Well, then," he said, still grinning, "It seems quite simple. I do have to say, I'm rather relieved."

"Me too," I said, smiling. I stood up as he moved toward the door. "Thank you for coming, Roger." I caught my breath, realizing how good it felt to have said his name out loud. "I really appreciate things being clear between us."

We smiled and shook hands one more time.

"It was lovely to meet you, Maria," Roger said quietly before turning and leaving the room. I felt my heart open and then close around the sound of my name on his lips. Shutting the door, I walked slowly to the window and stared through new eyes at the photographs I had hung there of our family, wondering if anyone else could see, as I did, the secrets beneath the smiles.

I WAS PACING back and forth in my room. Outside, light gray clouds that earlier in the day spit the morning's mist had now, two hours after dinnertime, come to a roiling boil. The air, charged with anticipation, began to spill fat drops of rain that spattered against the windows. Then, as if on cue, there was a loud crack of thunder as a streak of lightning split the sky.

A freshly popped bag of popcorn was filling my room with its buttery scent. I had carried it up from the kitchen a few minutes earlier, thinking I might take it up to Roger's room and offer to share it with him. But each time I headed toward the door, second thoughts kept stopping me in my tracks. I felt foolish for making such a big deal out of such a simple thing. After all, I reasoned, it was only popcorn. And yet, sitting now on the edge of my bed, my heart was pounding as if I were about to do something wrong.

Closing my eyes, I wanted to cry. I thought of other times in my life when I had talked myself out of doing something new, something exciting or slightly dangerous, because I was afraid of what others might think or what I imagined might happen. I realized now that I had more regrets about things I had wanted to do but hadn't, than regrets about things I had. I thought about the self-consciousness I'd felt earlier in relation to Roger, and knew I was tired of being so careful, of feeling frightened, immature, and small. The strong, confident woman I had been, walking to the mailbox today, would not be afraid to take chances in her life, would not hesitate to knock on the door of Roger's room.

Unraveled

Gathering my courage, I picked up the bag of popcorn, and glanced at my image in the mirror. My cheeks were flushed with excitement, my eyes alive and clear. I felt a wave of elation rising in my chest as I pulled open the door and stepped into the hall.

A COLONIAL IN THE SUBURBS

CLAUDE WAS DUE home from work any minute, and everything was ready. Will and Hannah were asleep in their beds, the table was set, and dinner was cooked and warming in the oven. Breathing a sigh of relief, I double-checked my image in the mirror, lit the candles in the center of the table, and put another log on the fire. Three months after settling into our new home in the suburbs of New Jersey, Claude and I had made a commitment to each other to begin this new life by making our marriage stronger, and I was more determined than ever to be the wife Claude needed me to be.

The incident in our family room in Ann Arbor had left both of us shaken and sober. Any problems we had experienced in our marriage until then paled in comparison to the violence we now realized we were capable of. Neither of us had yet pointed a finger of blame at the other. In fact, we had barely discussed it. The cause, I knew, was much deeper than the

Unraveled

specifics of that single incident, and some part of me was afraid that speaking the horror aloud would only make it more real. What we had done was to schedule an emergency counseling session with the minister of our church and taken time out of our packing to return for another session a few days later.

The minister hadn't seemed as alarmed as the two of us were. He had suggested that as a couple we were under a great deal of strain, having experienced so many changes in our lives in the past year, not least of which was our impending move. He had recommended that we make a point to spend more time together, to put the kids down early to bed before the two of us ate dinner, and to hire a babysitter once a week so we could go out. Looking back, I remember the way Claude and I had held hands throughout the counseling sessions, too frightened to let go. Although the minister obviously hadn't seen it, I suspected that our darker secrets, the real source of our problems, were buried beneath our shared fear of losing the only stability we knew.

Now, sitting on the sofa in the middle of the living room, waiting for Claude, I wanted to believe that this move was the new beginning we both needed. Claude now had a job he felt truly excited about, and because of his increased income, we had been able to afford a beautiful house, a split-level colonial in the suburbs of New Jersey, bigger and more formal than the tiny Cape Cod in Ann Arbor we had grown used to. Fair Haven, the borough where we now lived, was affluent, family-oriented, and small enough that, until they reached high school, the kids could walk to school. Our house was situated just two blocks from McCarter Pond, where Canada geese returned each spring to hatch and raise their goslings and neighborhood kids went fishing in the summer and ice-skated in the winter. It seemed the picture-perfect place for the picture-perfect family we still wanted to be.

The headlights of a car swept across the darkened living room. I stood up and looked out the front window in time to see Claude's car pulling into the drive. I glanced once more in the mirror and moistened my lips. Pasting a cheerful smile on my face, I waited for Claude to walk through the door. I wanted so desperately for things to work out between us, I chose to ignore the unmistakable feeling that I was standing in someone else's living room, in someone else's dream.

A NEW LIFE

I COULD HEAR WILL, *now five years old, and his friend Jeff, giggling and teasing each other as they wrestled in the family room. Hannah was toddling around the kitchen, opening and closing the cupboard doors, while I unloaded the dishwasher and kept one eye on the casserole in the oven. It had been just over a year since we had moved to New Jersey, but I could hardly remember the life we had once lived in Ann Arbor. My days now were scheduled around Will's preschool schedule, numerous after-school activities, and Hannah's play dates.*

"Mom, me and Jeff want to go fishing at the pond," Will shouted, as the two boys and their commotion raced up the stairs. "Can you take us, please, please?"

I glanced around at the still messy kitchen before turning to him.

"I'm sorry, buddy. I'm really busy," I said. Jeff looked quickly down at his shoes, but Will couldn't disguise his disappointment.

"Please, Mom. You're always *busy*," he said, pleading. I sighed, knowing it was true. But it wasn't easy keeping everything in order the way I liked it and Claude expected it to be. The too recent memory of Claude standing in front of me, yelling, "I expect you to take PRIDE in this house. I want RESULTS! Trying is NOT enough!" still resonated in me. I thought about the unfolded laundry piled in the middle of our bed, and the stacks of bills waiting to be paid.

"I'm sorry, Will," I said, truly meaning it. "I can't take you to the pond right now. I have too many things to do." Tears started to well up in Will's eyes as he slowly turned and motioned for Jeff to follow him back down the stairs. I felt as if a stone had lodged itself in my stomach, as I glumly wetted the sponge and began wiping the kitchen countertop. It was possible, I realized as I cleaned, that I simply wasn't capable of being everything I needed to be. I couldn't manage to keep a tidy, efficiently run house, be an attentive, caring wife, and a good mother. Even admitting the possibility, I was filled with a sense of relief.

"Okay," I said to myself, out loud, "if you can do only some things well, why not start with what matters most!"

Wiping my hands on the dish towel, I took the half-cooked casserole out of the oven, and then lifted Hannah onto my hip. "Come on, Missy," I said, "We have things to do. We're going for a walk to feed the ducks while Big Brother and Jeff fish."

Unraveled

An hour later, I was sitting on a bench by the pond, lifting my face to catch the last rays of the afternoon sun. Hannah was digging in the dirt not far from me, while Will and Jeff patiently cast their lines into the water, occasionally catching and releasing small, whiskered catfish, but mostly reeling in clumps of slimy green seaweed. Listening to the happy chatter of the boys, I felt more relaxed, happy, and patient than I had in a long time. I had already forgotten the unfinished tasks waiting for me, and willed myself not to think about whether or not Claude would accuse me of being lazy and undisciplined when he got home.

Instead, I began to wonder what my life would be like if it wasn't as rigidly structured as I had come to believe it should be. Staring past the far edge of the pond, I allowed myself only a whiff of a moment to imagine what it might be like if I were to start a new life with my children and no longer had to worry about what did and didn't work for Claude.

WEDNESDAY

I CARRIED THE TRAY with my breakfast of sliced apples, coffee, and toast up the stairs. Turning the corner, I noticed a small book leaning against the wall outside my door. It was a collection of poetry I loved. I smiled, realizing it was from Roger.

The night before, although Roger had declined my offer of popcorn, he had invited me in. His room was a suite, with a living room, small kitchen, and a bedroom loft. Stacks of books, dirty cups and glasses, and scribbled-on sheets of paper covered every flat surface. Roger had quickly cleared a spot for me on the couch, and then offered me a cup of tea. I had watched while he filled the kettle with cold water and lit the gas stove. Any nervousness between us had evaporated in laughter, when Roger, having filled the teapot with hot water and Earl Gray tea, tried to cover the teapot with a quilted toaster cover, having mistaken it for a tea cozy.

Sitting across from each other, me on the couch and

him on a chair, I had taken a sip of the tea Roger had made. My face must have registered my surprise.

"I hope it tastes okay," Roger said quickly. "Being English, I automatically put milk in it."

"It's good," I said, suddenly feeling self-conscious and particularly unsophisticated that microwave popcorn was the best I had come up with.

Soon, though, my flush of embarrassment had been completely forgotten. Roger began to tell me more of the story of his life, and then listened attentively and asked many questions about me and mine. It was easy to speak with him, and I trusted the sense of simplicity and openness between us. Our stories overlapped only in that he was married and divorced once and was the father of a twenty-three-year-old son. Our age difference—he was fifty-three to my thirty-five—felt less a gap than the fact that he had lived all of his life in England, exploring, writing, and taking photographs in exotic parts of the world like Africa and India, while I, except for a ride over the Mexican border once with Claude's parents, had never left the United States.

Telling my story, seeing my self and my own life in relief against his, afforded me a different perspective of all I had and hadn't done. I felt proud of what I had achieved, and of what Claude and I had done together. Being married, having children with a man I loved, and surviving Hannah's death were things that truly mattered to me. Rather than feeling I had missed out on a more exciting life, I realized that regardless of what I might or might not do in the months and years ahead, everything I had done had a place, and I felt proud and grateful for what I had experienced so far.

Just before midnight, as I stood up to leave, Roger had reached for a book lying on top of a stack on his desk. Thumbing through its pages, he had stopped, balanced his reading glasses on the end of his nose, and then read a poem, "The Journey," by Mary Oliver, aloud. Now, standing in the middle of the hall, I flipped through the pages and read the same words again:

> *"One day you finally knew*
> *what you had to do, and began . . ."*

Closing my eyes, I felt the same shudder of recognition I had felt the night before. Although I trusted that my life so far had been exactly as it needed to be, I also knew that newly discovered and yet unexpressed parts of myself were emerging, and I hadn't realized until now how strong and determined they were.

THE RHYTHMIC CREAK of the old porch swing and the scratch of my pen across the page kept me company as I rocked and filled my journal with thoughts. The air was mostly still, except for an occasional breeze; the sun made a dappled lawn of light on the forest floor. Pausing, my pen in midair, I watched a tiny brown mouse peek out from behind a log in the woodpile, then scamper to the safe haven of an overturned tin bucket across the yard. Except for the fact that my kids were not here, it was, for me, a perfect day.

I had decided to spend the afternoon at Thoreau, one of the retreat center's single-room cabins in the woods. The pioneer woman in me had always wanted to live surrounded by trees in a simple log home. Now, listening to the whispering leaves and feeling the integrity of an oak floor underfoot, I could feel traces of that dream returning. Everything about this place felt comforting and familiar to me.

Standing up from the swing, I slid my pen into the binding of my journal and opened the cabin's screen door. Inside, a twin bed, covered with a yellow chenille bedspread, a pile of pillows, and a folded patchwork quilt, was shoved lengthwise along the bottom of one window, serving both as the cabin's bed and sofa. A wooden rocking chair with one spindle missing, a distressed pine table with a checked tablecloth and kerosene lamp, and a single ladder-backed chair were the only other furnishings in the room.

In one corner, wooden planks nailed to the wall held an assortment of mismatched plates, glasses, a bowl, a few utensils, and assorted boxes of tea. Beneath the shelves stood a two-burner gas stove with a teakettle on top, a simple plywood counter, and a chipped porcelain sink. There was a well-worn broom leaning against the wall and a bottle of soap and a roll of paper towels under the sink. But, judging by the cobwebs clinging to the ceiling and the pine needles on the floor, no one had seen a need to do much cleaning here for quite some time, and I saw no reason to disagree.

Unpacking my backpack, I set the table for lunch: a chunk of fresh bread, several slices of sharp cheddar cheese, and a bright red tomato, sliced, that I'd picked as I passed the garden on my way to the cabin. While I ate, the water came to a boil in the teakettle on the stove. A mug of chamomile tea perfectly complemented the soft, melted chocolate bar I'd brought for dessert. While washing the single plate I'd dirtied and wiping the tablecloth clean, I thought about my other life, with its shelves of cookbooks, recipe card files, and weekly menus, carefully planned and taped to the refrigerator door. I had almost forgotten how delicious a simple meal, much less a simpler life, could be.

THE EVENING AIR was thick with the residue of the afternoon's heat as we made our way carefully along the path cut into the tall grass, me in front, Roger following.

During dinner, the two of us had, with comical combinations of finger pointing and nods, mimed an agreement to take a walk together after. I loved that the most important scheduling decision I had made all day had been this single, spontaneous one.

Before leaving the barn, Roger had wrapped a billowy silk scarf around my head to ward off mosquitoes. I had buried my nose in it, inhaling a musky cinnamon scent. Smiling, he had said, "I knew it would look beautiful on you. I brought it back with me from India." Then he continued, "If you don't mind, I have what might sound like a strange request. I'd like to share this walk with you in silence."

Now, wearing the scarf, picking my way into the twilight of the day, I felt grateful for the quiet. Although I had always loved the experience of silence when I was on my own, this was the first time I could remember, outside of church, that the silence between me and someone else was intentional rather than uncomfortable. It felt more like a fullness than an absence, and allowed me to see the way part of my mind kept coming up with things it wanted me to tell Roger. I hadn't realized before how much of my interaction with other people was social. It explained why I came away from so many conversations feeling exhausted and empty; in truth, nothing much had been said.

Cresting one of the taller hills, the two of us paused

and turned. Below, the retreat center's gray weathered barn was the tiniest dark ship in an ocean of waving, yellow grass. We stood together, watching the shadows deepen as the light faded from the landscape. Finally, turning, Roger took the lead as we began the long walk back to the barn.

I followed slowly, feeling like a woman from some other, exotic place. As the evening breeze lifted the edges of my scarf from my face, I imagined myself on one of Roger's journeys, walking in silence through the Sahara desert, in the tracks of the bedouin and their camels. I felt as if part of me already knew what it was like to lay on the sand, watching the moon rise into an African night sky, covered by a nomad's wool blanket.

As we neared the barn, Roger stopped in the middle of the path. The two of us stood, not speaking, our chins raised toward the stars. I smiled, appreciating how unexpectedly familiar everything in this moment felt. Although I was not facing him, I felt the shift in Roger's gaze as his eyes began to seek my face. Turning, I felt a question, without thought, completely unbidden, rise out of my heart.

"Haven't you recognized me yet?" I asked.

DARK SIDE OF THE MOON

HANNAH WAS LYING *in the hospital bed, sleeping peace-fully for the first time in days. The painkillers, coursing through the IV line into a vein in her left arm, made sure of that. Claude and I, our eyes red from too much crying and not enough sleep, sat in chairs on either side of the bed, staring blankly at each other and her. Although I could trace every mo-ment back from this one, I still couldn't believe we were here. It was as if we had warped into another dimension of reality, a reality no one would willingly enter. Claude and I hadn't yet had time to allow what was happening to sink into our bones, but we knew, from studying the serious faces on the doctors and nurses who had already spoken to us, that whatever was hap-pening with Hannah, it wasn't good.*

The door to the hallway opened, and one of the doctors we recognized, Hannah's pediatrician, Dr. Edman, motioned for us to join him in the hall. I glanced quickly at Hannah before rising, wanting to make sure she wasn't going to wake up and panic when she realized we were gone. She looked so tiny in the middle of the hospital bed, her skin translucent in the half-light. Kissing her lightly on the cheek, I whispered, "Daddy and I will be just outside in the hall." She didn't even stir.

Standing up and following Claude and Dr. Edman out of the room, I felt unsteady on my feet, but strong and determined inside. Whatever was wrong with Hannah, I knew we would do whatever needed to be done to fix it. Looking at Claude in the glaring fluorescent light of the hospital corridor, though, he seemed less certain. His eyes kept darting from the doctor's face, to mine, and then to the busy nurses who were readying carts with charts, syringes, and doses of morning medications.

Dr. Edman led us into an empty room next door to Hannah's. He perched on the edge of the bed, leaving the chairs for Claude and me. We each sat down. I inched my chair closer to Claude's and reached out to hold his hand. Any animosity or distance between us had disappeared in the time since we'd brought Hannah into the emergency room with blood in her urine the day before. The possibility that Hannah might be seriously ill had catapulted us beyond our own small concerns.

Dr. Edman cleared his throat. "The X-rays we took yesterday confirmed that there is a mass in Hannah's abdomen. We can't know much more than that until we do a biopsy. I'm going to schedule her for emergency surgery this week. Hopefully the surgeon will be able to remove the whole tumor. Even if he can't, we'll be able to send a piece of it to the lab, and then we'll know more."

A tumor. It was a word I had heard before, but I could never have imagined it was something that could grow inside an almost-three-year-old girl, much less my own daughter. I searched Dr. Edman's eyes, looking for clues to what it might mean. I didn't even want to ask the question that rose up in me at the sound of the word on his lips, but I couldn't stop myself.

"Does a tumor mean cancer?" I asked. Claude's body swung around to face me, and although I was still looking at Dr. Edman, I caught a glimpse of the horror in Claude's eyes. I couldn't be sure if he was angry with me for having spoken the dreaded word out loud, or if he was stunned because he hadn't yet thought of the possibility. In either case, it didn't matter to me. I had to know what we were dealing with, so I'd know how best to help Hannah.

Dr. Edman didn't answer right away. Finally he spoke. "A tumor doesn't necessarily mean cancer," he began, " but in this case, it very likely is. We know it's grown significantly in a short period of time. As you told us, when you took her to the emergency room in Michigan a few weeks ago while you were on vacation and Hannah was complaining that her stomach hurt, the doctors there could find nothing wrong. This tumor, as it is now, is about the size of a small soccer ball. If it had been this large three weeks ago, the doctors wouldn't have missed it."

Dr. Edman's voice was steady and measured, and I felt myself wanting to resonate with his calm, despite the clambering, shrieking voices in my mind that wanted me to collapse on the floor. I had so many questions, but I also understood that Dr. Edman was telling us they couldn't know anything of substance until they had opened Hannah up. Suddenly, the image of Hannah sedated on an operating table floated before my eyes, and I began to shake. Claude squeezed my hand and laid his arm across my shoulder. I leaned into him and immediately felt my sense of balance returning.

"Can you tell us why they might not be able to take the tumor out?" Claude asked.

"Well," Dr. Edman responded, "there's a chance, because it's so large, that it may have infiltrated one or more of the surrounding organs. We already know, for example, that we're going to have to remove at least all or part of one organ. The tumor seems to have grown out of Hannah's left kidney."

A bomb exploded in my gut. I felt Claude's body contract. I closed my eyes, desperate to wake up from the hellish realm we had just entered, but all I could see was the image of my body, crumpled on the family room floor, and Hannah, on the stairs, watching. It was as if I, looking through a wide-angle lens, had been afforded a new, even more terrible perspective on the thread connecting the story of our lives. It was only a little more than a year before when I had gone to the emergency room with blood in my urine from an injury to my left kidney.

DADDY'S GIRL

HANNAH WAS SITTING *on my lap in the wheelchair, playing with my hair and kissing my cheeks. I stared into her eyes, wanting to absorb the love and tenderness I saw there. She was hooked up to an IV pole, which she was now able to maneuver deftly as it followed her like a shadow wherever she went. Her head was mostly bald, except for a few wisps of blond hair, and her body was thin and weak, side effects from the chemotherapy drugs she had been receiving as part of the bone marrow transplant protocol. The two of us had been living in the hospital for more than a month, mostly in isolation, on the pediatric oncology floor. There was a sense of elation both of us felt now that her immune system had recovered sufficiently enough for her to be able to come out of her room.*

It had been five months since Hannah had been diagnosed with a rhabdoid tumor of the kidney. The doctors had been honest with us that the chances of survival beyond fifteen months were slim. Even so, we had begun treatment immediately, and when she relapsed less than two months later, we agreed to the bone marrow transplant. Claude and I had also insisted that Hannah be allowed to attend preschool, gymnastics class, and participate as a three-year-old in life as much as she was willing and able.

For her part, Hannah had been an inspiration to everyone around her. Acclimating quickly to life in the hospital, she had demanded that doctors and nurses introduce themselves to her using their "real" first names, and had become known as the "little girl with the red shoes" because she insisted on wearing her new red patent leather Mary Janes everywhere, even to surgery. The reason both of us were sitting in the same wheelchair now was that Hannah had requested, before leaving her hospital room, that the nurses bring a "grown-up" chair large enough to hold both of us so she could ride to her MRI sitting on her mommy's lap.

Now, as the two of us waited for the nurse to escort us into the darkened room where the MRI machine was, I prayed that Claude would arrive in time. He had promised Hannah earlier, on the phone, that he'd leave work and make the long drive to the hospital to ride into the MRI machine with her. But I knew that the project he was contributing to was months overdue, and Claude's manager and team members were relying heavily on his expertise.

It had helped that his parents had come from Michigan to be with Will and take care of the house for the six weeks Hannah and I were away, but even so, I knew Claude was under a lot of pressure from all sides, and I couldn't help wondering how long he could go on. I also knew that none of this would mean anything to Hannah, as the MRI was the test that frightened her the most. And she and I both understood that while I could watch what was happening from the control room, because I was already several months pregnant, I could not go in the machine with her.

The news of my pregnancy had been received with a mixture of amazement and disbelief by most of the people in our lives, but Claude, Will, Hannah, and I couldn't have been more thrilled. We wanted this baby. Watching Hannah's sedated body being wheeled into her first surgery, we had clung to each other, in the semi-privacy of a curtained alcove in the waiting room, and known without question that whatever the problems between us, our children mattered more to us than anything else, and we wanted, needed, to have more. Three months later, my pregnancy test had come back positive, and we had shared the joyous news with a beaming Will and Hannah on Christmas Day.

Now, although I was trying not to alarm Hannah, I couldn't help glancing anxiously toward the door at the end of the corridor. Hannah stroked my face with her small hands. "Don't worry, Mommy. Daddy will come. He told me. I know."

Just then, the door at the end of the hall opened, and Claude came striding through. Hannah turned and shrieked,

"Daddy," extending her arms toward him. Claude, grinning from ear to ear, broke into a trot. Reaching us, he scooped Hannah gently off my lap, and buried his face in her neck.

"I knew you would come, Daddy," Hannah said. Claude looked at me over Hannah's shoulder. We both had tears in our eyes.

"I love you, Missy Hannah," he said, his voice choked with emotion. "Nothing could stop me from being with you here."

I smiled at him, grateful and relieved. Bending down, with Hannah still in his arms, Claude gave me a kiss.

"How are you feeling? How's our baby doing?" he asked. I placed my hand on my stomach.

"I'm just a little tired, but everything seems great," I said.

The door to the MRI room opened, and a nurse motioned in our direction. I stood up from the wheelchair and pushed Hannah's IV pole behind Claude, who carried Hannah into the darkened room with its single, soft light above the control panel. The technician held open the door to the MRI machine, and I watched Claude and Hannah through the glass window as they went in. Claude gently laid Hannah on her back on the narrow board, while the technician wrapped Velcro straps around Hannah's head, arms, and legs to keep her still.

As soon as she was situated, Claude folded his six-foot, six-inch frame almost in half, and lay on his side on the same narrow board, just below Hannah's feet. I caught my breath and tried not to cry as I watched Hannah move one of her hands slightly so her fingers could touch the top of Claude's head. The technician double-checked everything, then turned and joined me in the control room, closing the door behind him. As he flicked a series of switches, a huge roar began building in the next room. As the magnetic drums inside the machine began to rotate, the platform Hannah and Claude were on slowly slid into the darkened chamber.

It seemed like hours, although I knew it was only minutes, while Hannah and Claude lay in the center of that terrifying roar. And though a part of me wanted to close my eyes to the frightening image, I also knew that moments like this mattered in a way so many others didn't. If I could imprint this image in my heart, I would never forget what Claude and I, together and separately, were willing to do for love.

Maria Housden

SEEN AND UNSEEN

THE ORGANIST WAS PLAYING the last bars of the opening hymn when the four of us entered the church and made our way quickly down the aisle. Claude, handsome in a suit and tie, carried Hannah in his arms, while Will and I, holding hands, followed closely behind.

Despite her illness, Hannah looked beautiful. She was wearing her favorite Easter dress, a white lace headband wrapped around her almost bald head, and her red patent leather shoes. Looking over her dad's shoulder, Hannah smiled and waved at Will and me. I smiled back, knowing I looked about as good as I could in my silk maternity dress, cheeks flushed with makeup and pregnancy's glow. Will glanced up at me, and I winked at him. He looked older than his six years in khaki trousers, a blue sport coat, and tie, and yet I was also aware of how small his fingers felt wrapped around mine.

Filing into an empty pew near the front of the sanctuary, the four of us sat down, Claude and I anchoring each end with

84

Will and Hannah in between. Digging into my purse, trying not to make too much noise because the pastor had begun speaking, I pulled out two boxes of raisins, a few blank pieces of paper, and a plastic bag of crayons.

"You're such a good mother, always so well prepared," the woman behind me, leaning forward, whispered in my ear. "It's a real treat to see such a nice family with children that are so well behaved."

I turned and smiled, grateful for the compliment, but wondering what the woman might have said if she had been with us that morning, listening to Claude and me bickering back and forth, yelling at our kids to get ready for church. I could never have imagined, before Hannah got sick, that life could return so quickly to normal. Within weeks of Hannah's and my return home from the hospital, our family had slipped into a more regular routine, which included the less than stellar dynamics between Claude and me. It was now clear that in the face of a crisis, Claude and I were capable of being on our best behavior, but as soon as the crisis was even temporarily averted, the residue of resentment between us floated again to the surface, unresolved.

Now, settling back into the pew, inhaling the sense of peace I always felt in the church's silence, I couldn't help wondering which was more true—the story of us sitting here, all together, the perfect family at church on Sunday morning, or the frustrated, angry life and lies nobody else could see?

EATING THE SUN

HANNAH DIDN'T LOOK AS SICK as the doctors said she was as she arranged the Oreos in two stacks on the plate in front of her. In the months since her bone marrow transplant, her hair had grown back, short and downy soft, her cheeks had become rounder and pink, and her strength had returned. This morning, on waking, she had clambered up the steps to our room and jumped in the middle of Claude and me in bed, exclaiming, "Mommy, I have the very, very best idea. Can me and Will have Oreo cookies for breakfast?"

Her eyes were so bright and mischievous, both Claude and I had laughed out loud, and with barely a second thought I had said, "Yes."

A month before, doctors had discovered another tumor in Hannah's abdomen. This time, though, it was inoperable. The only treatment options available now were highly experimental and would require Hannah to spend every day of what remained of her life in the hospital, with no guarantee of remission. Claude and I were sick with despair but in agreement about what was best for Hannah; with leaden hearts we had told Hannah's doctors we were taking Hannah home and would not subject her to any more treatment.

Claude had continued to pray every night for a miracle, as he had ever since Hannah's diagnosis. And while I held my heart open to every possibility, I also felt that the best I could offer our family was my willingness to be both honest and practical about what needed to be done next. No one could tell us exactly how much longer Hannah would be alive, whether she would be able to hold our new baby, due in three months, or celebrate her fourth birthday, which was four months away. Any estimate the doctors could give was at best a guess.

We had broken the news to Will and Hannah as gently and age-appropriately as possible, telling them that the lump in Hannah's tummy had returned and this time the doctors couldn't take it out. Although many people had disagreed with our decision to be honest with our children about what was happening, I felt strongly and Claude had agreed that Will and Hannah deserved an opportunity to discuss the truth of the situation with us rather than trying to guess what was happening or to overhear it from someone else.

But even I was unprepared for their reactions. Will had hugged me and then hugged Hannah, thanking me for telling him so that, knowing Hannah was going to die, he could now make a point to be especially nice to her every day she was alive. Hannah, in her own extraordinary way, had immediately announced that she was going to heaven to be with God and his angels, and that what she wanted more than anything was to be able to see her new baby sister or brother and to die at home, in the bed that smelled like her mom and dad.

Now, as I puttered around the kitchen and listened to Will's and Hannah's happy chatter, I felt grateful for having agreed to the cookies-for-breakfast diet. As I poured a second glass of milk for each of them, I heard the doorbell ring downstairs. I called down, "Come in, the door's open," and smiled when I saw it was Rhea, Jeff's mom, and Jacqueline, Jeff's little sister, who was the same age as Hannah and one of Hannah's best friends. The two of them came up the steps into the kitchen, and when they saw the chocolaty happiness on Will's and Hannah's faces, Jacqueline's eyes lit up, but Rhea didn't look so sure.

"We're having cookies for breakfast," Hannah announced proudly. "Do you want some, Jackie?" she asked, holding several cookies in her hand, gesturing for Jacqueline to take them. Jacqueline turned to her mother.

"Can I, please Mom?" she pleaded.

"I don't know. Cookies for breakfast?" Rhea asked, looking at me.

For a moment I wondered if I had, as a mother, once again goofed. For months, several people, one of them a very close friend of mine, had suggested it was irresponsible of me not to put Hannah on an all-organic, macrobiotic diet. At the time, while I had agreed that for some people with cancer it might be the right decision, I had felt that Hannah was too young to be subjected to such a rigorous regimen, especially since eating was one of the few pleasures that remained to her. Now, though, the part of me that had always wanted to believe there was something we could do to save Hannah, was saying, "I told you so" and poking me in the ribs.

Hannah, perhaps sensing my wavering confidence, let out a loud guffaw. "What's the big deal?" She laughed, handing the stack of cookies to Jacqueline. "They're just cookies. Go ahead, it's okay."

It was like one of those moments in the movies, when the clouds part and the light shines through. They were just cookies, but this wasn't just any day. This was a day when Hannah was happy and sick, when she and her brother were loving each other and covered in chocolate. I knew that we needed to inhale these miraculous, joyful moments with Hannah, the way plants eat the sun all summer in order to survive the long winter months ahead.

Maria Housden

THURSDAY

MY FACE WAS CLOSE enough to the freshly mown grass to inhale its sweet scent and notice that blades not yet touched by the morning sun were still strung with pearls of dew. I'd woken early, and after a small breakfast and a half hour of prayer in the chapel, I had packed my journal, an orange, two granola bars, and a bottle of water in a paper sack, rolled my quilt into a manageable roll, and carried everything along a path to a circle of cut grass on the crown of one of the hills.

Lying on my stomach, my chin in my hands, I watched birds dart in and out of the grass, chasing insects with iridescent wings. Below, a farmer and his tractor made back-and-forth furrows, while above, trailing white ribbons tracked silvery airplanes across the bowl of blue sky. I forgot all about my journal and the things I'd come here to think about, and instead, laying my hand in the crook of my arm, concentrated on the warmth of the morning sun on the backs of my legs and tried to notice everything I might not otherwise have seen.

I hadn't even realized I was asleep, until, drifting up, I felt myself drawn into consciousness by the presence of another. Keeping my eyes closed and careful not to be distracted by the sounds of crickets and buzzing insects in the grass, I allowed myself to drift in the darkness behind my eyes until, gradually, the image of a woman began to emerge.

She was standing, with her arms outstretched, beckoning me. Tall, like me, but older by about thirty years, she was beautiful in the way that a woman with confidence is, her gaze strong and tender at the same time. Her face unapologetically wore the lines of one who has loved deeply and is still loved, of one who has known pain and grief without running from either. I could feel that she was stronger than me, and more graceful, too, willing not to have all the answers. I knew, in a way you can know only in dreams, that this woman liked to write and paint, that she enjoyed her work, and that now, although her home was often filled with the laughter and voices of family and friends, except for her big dog, she lived mostly on her own.

Moving toward her embrace, I felt curiously at peace. As she wrapped her strong, life-lived arms around me, she said quietly in my ear, "It's okay, honey, don't worry, it's going to be all right."

As soon as I heard her voice, I knew. This woman, who was holding me in her arms with so much under-standing and compassion, was the woman I was going to become. Everything I was going to be, this woman al-ready was. She loved me, cared for me, and was able to look at me with such unconditional regard because she had been me, had been where I was now. I realized then, just as I had in the first moment of meeting Roger, that at some level I wasn't going to have to figure out whether to do this or that in my life. Everything that needed to happen would happen, and everything that needed to be done would be done.

I WAS SITTING at the desk in my room, holding a pen in my hand, staring out the window. I had returned from my nap on the hill too late for lunch, but Mary had left a plate with sliced cucumber, bran muffins, and a scoop of fresh corn-and-pepper salad in the refrigerator for me. The plate lay empty on the desk beside me now, the meal already forgotten as I searched for words to de-scribe the feeling of the dream I'd had of the woman I was going to become.

It felt necessary, important somehow, to allow mo-ments like this to refilter through me so that I might capture them on the page. These days an almost constant stream of memories was pouring through me, and powerful images and realizations were coming to me in dreams. I was beginning to understand that perspective was one of the things that had, until now, been missing in my life, and I would need, in the future, to remind myself of the lessons I was learning now.

Suddenly, a steady, piercing tone cut the air. A fire alarm! I jumped up, knowing I should head straight outside, but instead, I raced up the stairs toward where the sound of the alarm was coming. Out of breath, I stopped in the center of the upstairs hall. Smoke was pouring from a crack under the door of Roger's room.

"Roger," I shouted, surprising myself with the level of panic in my voice. Bursting through the door, I almost ran into Roger, who was standing in the middle of the living room, waving a dish towel in each hand; a burnt black bagel half lay on its side on the kitchen counter.

"I was trying to toast it over the burner on the gas stove," Roger explained sheepishly. "Then I got involved in my writing and forgot."

Roger looked so helpless standing there, bare-chested, in running shorts, two faded dish towels in his hands, that I couldn't help it. I began to laugh.

"Oh my God, in a barn made of wood, I was sure we were goners!" I said.

"What a disaster," Roger said, laughing now too. As I

stood on my tiptoes to remove the battery from the droning smoke detector, he opened the remaining windows and fanned the rest of the smoke out of the room. Finally, when we were finished, he turned to me.

"If you'd like," he said, still smiling, "I think I could manage, without too much problem, to make us some coffee."

"Yes, that would be lovely," I said.

I watched while he pulled the coffeemaker toward him, dumped an unmeasured portion of coffee in the filter, and then poured an equally unmeasured amount of water from the teapot on the stove into the coffee maker's reservoir.

"Shouldn't you pay attention to how much coffee and water you're using?" I asked, as diplomatically as I could.

Roger turned away from what he was doing to look at me and, seeing the concerned look on my face, grinned.

"I never measure anything," he said, his eyes dancing. "That way, it's always a surprise!"

I felt a door open unexpectedly in me. There was no way I would ever have thought of it that way. While he continued to busy himself in the kitchen, I excused myself to go to the bathroom. Washing my hands, I noticed his black leather shaving bag on the counter next to the sink. I hesitated only a moment before taking a peek:

a well-worn toothbrush, toothpaste, a tube of Kiehl's moisturizing lotion, a tiny bottle of tea rose oil, Body Shop deodorant, and a bottle of Eternity, a cologne.

Returning to the living room, I sat on the couch, while Roger carefully carried two mugs of coffee from the kitchen. As he handed me mine, our fingers brushed each other, and I felt a rush of energy, like electricity, run up my arm. It was so unexpected that I instantly felt self-conscious and bent my head quickly to take a sip. Roger sat down, and although no part of our bodies was touching, there was an energy, like warmth, jumping back and forth between us.

I felt Roger's eyes on me, his glance lingering, thoughtfully watching. Finally, I raised my head and looked at him. I noticed the smile lines etched into his face, the light stubble of gray along his chin, and the way he cradled the mug in his big hands. Feeling my heart swell with gratitude, I smiled at him.

IT WAS ALMOST DARK, but there was enough light to see that everything in the room was just the way I'd left it. The chairs had been moved to one side, leaving a large open space on the floor, and a small vase of wild-flowers stood, surrounded by the three white votive candles, in the center of the altar. I lit the candles, their flickering light reflected off the gold, green, and blue of the stained-glass window. Roger, who had paused for a moment, just inside the doorway, said softly, "Oh, Maria. Thank you for bringing me here. It is exquisite."

I smiled, gesturing for him to join me. The two of us stood for a moment, watching the candlelight and shadows dance on the walls, then kneeled side by side in front of the altar. I turned to look at Roger. His eyes were already closed, his hands laid, palms down, on his knees. I studied his profile, its strong, chiseled features, eyelashes curling up against his cheek, and the half-smile on his lips. Then, turning back to look at the cross hanging from the ceiling, I closed my eyes too. Inhaling deeply, then exhaling in a long, drawn-out breath, I felt my body relax and soften, realizing that, in this moment, I did not wish for anything else. Everything I loved, everything I had ever been or would someday be was a part of the air I was now breathing. I closed my eyes and said a prayer silently in my heart.

"Thank you, thank you, thank you, God, for this moment, for this place, for this life. May I remember, too, that everything that has happened until now, including Hannah's death, is a part of this moment I am now living, and had to happen in order to bring me here."

I felt my body continue to settle into itself, my awareness becoming singularly focused on the slow, steady beat of my heart, the rise and fall of my breath. I lost track of time and of Roger's presence beside me. As my thoughts became like clouds across a summer sky, wafting through my mind, untouched, my sense of my self became more an energetic aliveness than a body, a separateness both independent from and connected to everything around me.

Gathering my attention, I knew without thinking that this feeling was the essence of who I was; it was the life energy that fueled my body as it moved through the story of my life. My time on retreat wasn't about Claude, my kids, or even Roger; it was about me returning to this awareness of myself, learning to trust my instincts as a woman, knowing that the most authentic expression of myself in my life could only, necessarily, be drawn from the source of this silence in me.

SILENCE

THE HOUSE WAS QUIET *and smelled like ice ripening. I wrote in my journal and watched Hannah breathe. Baby Margaret was asleep on the bed next to Hannah. Her birth, exactly three weeks earlier, had seemed a bittersweet impossibility as it unfolded before our eyes. Hannah had been thrilled, and insisted on coming to the hospital. "It's what big sisters do," she'd said. Although we couldn't have known it then, it turned out to be the last day Hannah left the house. The next day, she had been in so much pain that, with the assistance of a hospice nurse, we started her on morphine.*

The circle of life had never been so evident to me. Even now, seeing Hannah's wasted body beside the plump pinkness of the little sister she had so desperately wanted, my heart felt as if it might split in two. These days, while Margaret mostly nursed and slept, Hannah lay with her eyes closed in the middle of Claude's and my bed, sleeping, barely speaking. Now, exhausted from too many sleepless nights, I closed my eyes and rocked, resting my head against the back of the chair.

Suddenly Hannah moaned. My eyes flew open. Hannah was reaching for me. I jumped up, checking the morphine pump and IV line to make sure nothing had malfunctioned.

"Does it hurt, baby?" I asked, stroking the top of her head. "Should I push the button and give you more morphine?"

Hannah nodded, still moaning and reaching for me. I pushed the button. I was starting to feel scared. Although her condition had seemed stable when Dr. Kamalaker stopped by yesterday, something had drastically changed. I decided to pick her up, not knowing what else to do. I lifted her up off the bed and sat on the edge of the mattress, resting her body on my lap. Placing a soft pillow between her head and my arm, I covered the rest of her with her pink blanket. Hannah stopped moaning. Although her breath sounded strange, rapid, and shallow, her eyes were open, looking at me. I reached for the phone and called Claude at work.

"I think you should come home right away," I said. Then I made two more calls: one to the hospice nurse, and one to my friend Kate, asking her to come to the house to help with Margaret and asking her to arrange for our friend Lili to bring Will, who was at Lili's house, playing with her son, Philippe.

Minutes later, I heard Kate's footsteps running up the stairs. When she opened the door and saw Hannah on my lap, she began to cry.

"Is this it?" she whispered.

"I don't know," I said. Kate picked up Margaret.

"We'll wait downstairs," she said. Just then the door opened and Pat, the hospice nurse, came in. Our eyes met, but neither of us said anything. She kneeled on the floor in front of me and gently examined Hannah, who was now thrashing intermittently. When she looked up, she had tears in her eyes, and I knew. Paging Hannah's doctor, Pat quietly explained what was happening, listened for a moment, nodding, and then hung up. There was another tentative knock on the door. Will stepped into the room. He looked at Hannah on my lap, and then at me.

"Is it time, Mom?" he asked.

"Yes, Will," I said.

Will bent down, stroked Hannah's hair, and kissed the top of her head.

"I love you, Hannah," he said. Her eyes rolled toward him. The two of them looked at each other for a moment, and then Will looked at me.

"Mom, I want to wait downstairs, but as soon as Hannah dies, come and get me, okay?"

I nodded. He kissed Hannah once more.

"Remember, Hannah, I love you," he said, then turned and left the room.

Ten minutes later, Claude's car pulled into the driveway. The door slammed. I heard his footsteps thudding on the stairs. He threw open the door.

"What's happening?" he asked Pat, who was sitting on the floor with the morphine pump.

"Hannah's dying," I said, more calmly than I could believe. "She's been waiting for you. You have to tell her it's okay to go."

Claude fell to his knees and let out a low moan. His body shook with sobs. He lifted his head, leaned over, and kissed her. Up until this moment, though he had agreed that I should speak with Will and Hannah about the fact that Hannah was likely to die, he had been unable to speak to Hannah or anyone else about the one thing he could not bear, saying good-bye.

"It's time for you to go, Missy," he said now. "Don't worry about us. We love you. We're going to be okay."

Although Hannah's body continued to fight for twenty more minutes, some part of her already felt free, as if the life force inside and outside her body was who she was; her body seemed a separate thing. Then, one moment she was alive and breathing, the next, she wasn't. I couldn't believe how unexpected it felt. I looked into her eyes. Nothing but blue. The room had filled with an almost palpable stillness that enveloped us in its thick, white peace.

FROZEN IN TIME

CLAUDE, WILL, AND I *were standing on the spot that would be Hannah's grave, gazing at the pond. We watched while one duck followed another across the surface of the water, and a slender white egret nosed its beak into the reeds along the far shore. I was holding baby Margaret, who was asleep in my arms, while Wanda, the cemetery manager, waited a discreet distance away.*

The three of us, Claude, Will, and I, were making an almost impossible decision; we were deciding if this was the right place for Hannah's body to be buried. And, if it was, this would be where Claude and I would be buried too. It was inconceivable to both of us that Hannah's body should spend eternity on its own. We had told Wanda we wanted three plots, so I could be buried next to Hannah after my death, and Claude could be buried next to me.

"I think this is the right place," Will said quietly, breaking the silence. "Hannah would like the pond, and my kids will

be able to throw stones and stuff when I bring them here to see Hannah." I bent down to give Will a hug, burying my face in his hair, not wanting him to see any more tears.

"What do you think?" Claude asked me. Looking at him, I wondered if the despair and resignation was as obvious in my eyes. I turned and looked again at slope of the land as it emerged from the stand of pines and rolled downhill toward the plateau where we stood and then on to the edge of the pond.

I appreciated the way this place didn't feel or look like a cemetery. Because the grave markers were laid flat on the ground, it looked more like a place for a picnic than a home for the dead. Everything about this spot spoke to me of another time, and I couldn't shake the feeling that I had been here before. Though Claude and I had decided to bury Hannah in Ann Arbor, because it was where Will and Hannah had been born, where Claude and I had lived in married housing while he was in graduate school, and where we had owned our first home, I couldn't remember ever having had a reason to visit a cemetery in the time we had lived here. I suspected that the feeling of familiarity was simply my way of trying to make it okay that we were planning to bury and leave Hannah's body in this spot, and then drive away.

"I think Will is right. Hannah would like it here," I said. Claude nodded his head in agreement and gave a thumbs-up sign to Wanda. I smiled gratefully at him. I knew he had really preferred the gravesite under the pines at the top of the hill, but we had agreed to let Will cast the final vote. There were so few things Will had been able to have a say in or control.

"Let's walk back through the pines before we return to the car," I said. Will let out a whoop and raced ahead up the hill. Filled with relief at having made such an enormous decision, Claude and I joined hands and began the climb. As we crested the hill and stepped into the shade of the trees, something about the bend of the pines, the slope of the hill, and the path through the trees touched a memory in me. I suddenly remembered that Claude and I had been here before, and knew why I hadn't fully realized it until now.

On a gray winter afternoon, more than ten years before, Claude had taken a break from his studies and invited me to go ice-skating with him on a pond he had noticed on his way home from class. Holding Claude's hand now, with Margaret in my other arm, and Will running up ahead, I could remember the feeling of my skates slung over my shoulder, the icy breath in my nostrils, and the chunks of snow dropping onto the path in front of us as we had made our way home through the trees.

I knew then that this was where Hannah's body should be—in a place that could hold not only Will's hopes for the future but also memories of a life Claude and I had known long ago.

BLANKET OF GRIEF

I WOKE in the middle of the night, not certain why. Opening my eyes, there was no light in the room. I lay quietly for a moment, and then realized what had woken me. Claude, lying next to me in the bed, was quietly sobbing into his pillow. Hearing him, I rolled toward him until my body was stretched alongside his. Lifting my arm from beneath the blankets and laying it across his chest, I felt his whole body begin shaking, as he knew I was awake and no longer had to subdue his tears.

There are no words for the dark spaces between breaths where Claude and I went in the first months and years after Hannah's death. Grief was a blanket that enveloped and suffocated us. Watching Hannah's casket being lowered into the ground, I had felt everything I knew or trusted about my self and my life fall away. The singleminded focus on Hannah and our family that I'd had in the last year of Hannah's life vanished. I was left, instead, with a sense that my mind had been completely disconnected from my body. And although Claude had returned to work a week and a half after Hannah died, caring for Margaret and Will was the best and only thing I seemed to be able to do.

"I think Hannah died because of me," Claude whispered now, as if the words were too terrible to say aloud. "I should have been a better person, closer to God. I prayed every day, but I started too late. It wasn't enough."

I began to cry too, as my own guilt and grief broke open in me. Although I had barely wanted to name the truth in my heart, I had felt, since the moment we heard Hannah's tumor was in her left kidney, that Hannah had sacrificed herself to the anger in me. How else could God justify taking such a pure and joyful life? Holding Claude's broken body in my arms, I felt breathless in the face of life's cruelty. I ached for what Claude, Will, and I now knew about the hopelessness and helplessness of being human and alive. And I ached for everything we would never know: why Hannah died and other children didn't, Hannah as a ballerina, Hannah at twelve.

"I've been thinking all this time it was my fault," I said, taking deep breaths between sobs in order to get the words out. "I can't forget the image of her on the steps to the family room that day. But I also can't believe that the God I love would punish us by punishing her. Maybe, if there is a reason, it's something we simply will not ever be able to understand."

"Well, I can't accept that there is no reason," Claude said.

Unraveled

"But I also know that Hannah would not want us to be angry because she died. I think the only thing we can do is try to be better people because we love Hannah, and because she was so good."

I understood how Claude felt. I had been praying ever since Hannah's death that each of us, having been stripped of everything that mattered except our children and each other, might somehow find a way to care about life again, to learn from our mistakes and shortcomings and become better partners, better parents. But I was afraid, too, that our guilt and anger in response to Hannah's death might have hardened our hearts and further widened the gap between us. Closing my eyes, feeling Claude's body next to mine, now softened and quiet, I felt comforted by his presence but broken open to a deeper loneliness too. I knew now that there was no assuaging another person's guilt or grief. And although Claude and I could not be more together in our shared suffering and missing Hannah, we also could not be more alone.

FRIDAY

I WATCHED AS THE SPIDER dangled precariously on her almost invisible thread, then swung wide, catching the outside edge of her web. I challenged myself to notice every detail of her movement, knowing there was beauty in each one. Finally, my eyes tired, I leaned back in the rocking chair in the shade of the cabin's porch roof and took a bite of my apple, grateful that I had decided to spend another day in the woods.

I was completely enjoying being on my own now, and savoring the way my thoughts could chase themselves from one point to the next, without any chance of being interrupted. I hadn't fully realized until now the way that, even as a young girl, my attention was always being diverted from what I thought was interesting or important. I had come to believe that it was my responsibility to respond with interest, even if it was feigned, to whatever my mother, father, husband, and children were interested in; my own thoughts took a backseat to everyone else's. Now, though, in the silence and solitude of these past few days, the movement of my thoughts was often more interesting than the specifics of the thoughts themselves.

And yet, as much as I loved being on my own, I also missed my kids. I had spoken to them and my sister several times in the past few days. Each time they had been happy to hear my voice, but were having too much fun to speak with me for long. Laura had assured me that the time was passing quickly for them and that everything was going well.

Even so, I found myself wondering about them, Claude, and even Roger. It seemed that, although I was obviously benefiting greatly from this stretch of time on my own, there was also a large part of me that loved relationship and being part of a community. I could see now that there wasn't only one thing I needed. Different movements, like tides, were continually shifting back and forth in me, running first toward wanting to be with another, and then slowly turning back toward a more solitary aloneness that wanted only to be on its own.

The way that Roger and I had met and become friends seemed only to reinforce that point. But what now seemed even more peculiar, or perhaps magical, was how each of us had ended up here during the same week. My sister Laura had offered at Christmas to give me the gift of the retreat I had been talking about for years. It was she and her manager at the bank who had determined that these ten days in July were the best time for her to take off work to watch my kids. I had made reservations to stay at The Hermitage after seeing a write-up about it in a library book.

Roger, on the other hand, had originally planned to stay for a month at another retreat center, just down the road. But a week before he was scheduled to leave, the center had called him to say they had mistakenly over-booked the first ten days of his stay. They had made reservations for him to stay at the The Hermitage for those ten days.

"No problem," Roger had said at the time, "as long as I have a quiet space in which to write, it makes no difference to me."

Now, rocking on the porch of the cabin, I could not ignore the synchronicity that had made our visits overlap in the same week; nor could I stop my mind from wondering what it might mean.

I STEPPED OUT of the shower and reached for a towel as drops of water slid down my back and legs onto the cool tile floor. The afternoon's humidity had chased me from the porch of the cabin. I wiped my body dry, wrapped the towel around my hair, brushed my teeth, and began smoothing lavender-scented lotion over my arms and legs. As my hands slid along my limbs, out of the corner of my eye, I saw my reflection in the mirror. Almost shyly, I turned and stood up straight. Mesmerized, I could not remember the last time I had really looked at my body.

My eyes traveled over my form, across my strong shoulders, past my small, soft breasts, touch-sensitive nipples, firm, flat stomach, and childbearing hips. I allowed my glance to linger on my triangle of pubic hair before continuing down toward my long, strong legs and solid, man-sized feet. Extending my hands, I studied them too. Of all the parts of my body, they were the most familiar; long, strong, and capable, they were not only the hands of a lover, mother, healer, and woman, they were the hands of a poet, gardener, explorer, writer, and painter.

Staring at the full length of myself in the mirror, I marveled that this body was capable not only of closing around my lover as he entered me, but that it had also opened wide to deliver four babies into the world. I thought of how, in the busyness of my days, I often willed my body not to need anything. Distracted by my compulsion to take care of everyone and everything else,

I often forgot to eat, refused to sit down, and willed my-self not to have to go to the bathroom for hours. See-ing my body now, I vowed I would take better care of myself.

"Thank you," I whispered, wanting to cry, except I was smiling too widely to make tears.

THE SETTING SUN was casting its blazing orange eye on the fields as I made my way back to the retreat center's barn. Swinging my backpack in one hand, I walked slowly, the way I imagined Native American Indians did, so as not to frighten the small animals, insects, and birds that kept darting across the path.

After a day of sitting on the front porch of the cabin, all my senses were heightened. The resonance of belong-ing I'd felt in the chapel the night before had expanded to include every living thing: the light, the sky, the earth, and the trees. I loved the way this place and time in my life was not only igniting important memories in me but also, as I had in the past day begun writing again, notes for the book about Hannah's life, it was clear that this place was inspiring me to move more wholly and fully in the direction of my unlived dreams.

Rounding the corner of the barn, I had about reached the door when I heard a shout. Turning, I saw

Roger running toward me, grinning and waving like a twelve-year-old kid. He must have spotted me from the window in his room. I had to laugh. More than once in the past couple of days, I had passed this way in the afternoon, secretly hoping he'd see me and come down. Now, when I had no such thought in my mind, it had finally happened.

"Hello, Maria!" he said breathlessly, giving me a quick hug. "I missed you at dinner this evening." He paused to catch his breath and then continued. "I was wondering, if you're not too tired and it's not too late, if you might like to amble."

I smiled, appreciating how handsome he looked, his expectant blue eyes twinkling at me.

"Sure, I'd love to," I said.

"Oh good! Here, let me take that for you," Roger replied, reaching for my backpack. He disappeared inside the barn. A few moments later, he returned.

"I put it on the floor in your room," he said.

"Thank you," I said, taking his hand. The two of us looked at each other and smiled. It now felt the simplest, most natural thing for my hand to be held in his.

The light of the moon served to guide us as we picked our way carefully along the path. For the next half hour, we walked in silence. Eventually, although we could no longer hold hands, as the path was too narrow

113

for us to walk side by side, I nonetheless felt particularly attuned to Roger's presence. Too soon, it seemed, we had completed the path's circle and returned to the barn. Before opening the door, Roger stopped and turned toward me. Although I could see only the outline of his form in the moonlight, I could feel his eyes traveling over me. My body began to tremble in anticipation. I was sure he could feel, as I could, the pounding of my heart in my chest as he moved close enough for us to inhale and exhale the same breath. Staring into my eyes without speaking, he slowly began to run his hands along the sides of my face, then over my shoulders, and arms, and finally, encircled my waist.

"Do you have any idea how beautiful you are?" he whispered. I felt my eyes fill with tears as I inhaled the muskiness of his scent.

Reaching my arms around his neck, I allowed him to pull me close. My lips could feel the warmth of his, but still they didn't touch. Like a slow-burning fire, Roger's fingers began to travel over the skin of my back, tracing the curve of my ribs and spine underneath my shirt.

"Thank you for this time we've had together," he said quietly, gently pulling away. "I think it's best, though, that we not ask for it to be more than this."

There was a roaring sound in my ears, as part of me,

drunk with an awareness of loving him, struggled to return to my body. My mind suspected he was probably right, but later as I lay in the dark of my room, my body was still trembling as I savored the memory of his heart beating against my chest.

Maria Housden

DANCING WITH LOVE

OUR BODIES WERE SWAYING back and forth to the music, having spontaneously come together as each of us was getting dressed and ready for the day. My arms were wrapped around Claude's neck, and his were pulling me close at the small of my back.

More than two and a half years after Hannah's death, it seemed a miracle that not only had Claude and I managed to regain our footing and reemerge into the world and each other, we had also created another new life between us. A little over a year after Hannah's death, our daughter Madelaine had been born. Deciding to get pregnant once more had been a huge decision for Claude and me to make. But both of us had felt strongly that without another baby, our family was incomplete. It had also felt as if our marriage and family had been opened to new sense of hope and possibility, having taken such an abrupt, unexpected turn.

Holding Madelaine for the first time, I had looked into Claude's teary eyes and known that she was the last baby we needed to have. I felt complete as a mother, and happier than I had ever been. Having negotiated such a dark path together, Claude and I had discovered a new respect for what we could accomplish as a team. He was the only person in the world who would ever appreciate how much I had lost and changed since Hannah's death. And after the loneliness and heartache I had experienced in my grief, the love we knew with each other and for Hannah, Will, Margaret, and Madelaine meant more to me than it ever had before.

I heard Will's footsteps pounding up the steps to our room, and then pause in the doorway. I turned my head to smile at him. He grinned, his eyes alive and shining as he watched Claude and me dance.

"Hey, buddy," Claude said, "do you want to join us?" Will nodded and then stepped shyly into our embrace, wrapping his arms around both our legs. As we held on to each other, the song we were dancing to ended and another began. The three of us continued to dance.

"This feels good," Will said, finally, giving our legs a squeeze. Claude and I laughed and kissed each other lightly. Then, readjusting his grip on my body, he whispered in my ear, "I wonder if it's time for us to start shopping for your new wedding ring."

I opened my eyes and looked into his. Smiling, I said teasingly, "Yes, and you can give it to me when we renew our vows."

Claude laughed and poked me in the ribs. This had become

our shared joke, that I'd begun to have an image of myself in a grown-up wedding with my kids as attendants, rather than the one Claude and I had had, with homemade bridesmaids' dresses in dusty rose satin, that I'd planned in my head when I was sixteen years old. Claude wasn't sure he was ready for another ceremony, but the one thing we did seem to agree on was that neither of us had ever been crazy about the setting of the thin white gold engagement ring Claude had given me when he proposed. He had explained, when he first slipped it onto my finger, that the small but beautiful diamond was what he had carefully chosen—the setting, he wanted me to choose. But I, ever the romantic at twenty years old, had insisted I wanted to wear the exact ring Claude had given me, even though I had always imagined my wedding ring as a thick yellow gold band.

Now, twirling together in the middle of our bedroom with Will's arms wrapped around our legs, I realized that renewing our vows or getting the ring I had always wanted really wasn't that important to me. What mattered was this life and family Claude and I were still creating together, and though it was far from perfect, I trusted that there was a movement wiser and greater than the strength of our shared or individual wills that was steering our relationship in the direction it needed to go.

Unraveled

RING OF FIRE

I RAN THE DUST RAG along the edge of Claude's dresser and underneath the homemade Styrofoam picture frame and photo of Will he had received as his first Father's Day gift when Will was a year old. There was one item on Claude's dresser, though, that I hesitated to touch. If I wasn't mistaken, Claude's white gold wedding band had been sitting in the exact same spot when I dusted a week before. Lifting the ring carefully off the surface of the dresser, its telltale imprint on the dusty surface told me what I needed to know. I felt sick to my stomach. There was no room in the story I had dreamed of my life for this.

Balancing the ring on the tip of my index finger, I listened to the sounds of Claude getting ready for work in the bathroom and the faint strains of cartoon music wafting up the stairs from the television room. One part of me wasn't surprised by this turn of events. Not long ago, Claude had turned forty. Soon after, he had purchased a weight-lifting machine and started *reading books from a list of one hundred classics, emphatically insisting that I should be reading them too.*

Inhaling a shaky breath, I was still trying to decide what to say, when the bathroom door opened. Claude stopped three steps in when he saw his wedding ring dangling from the finger of my right hand. His face was expressionless as he stared at me.

"You haven't been wearing it, have you?" I asked quietly. He didn't respond, not even a nod. The two of us continued to stare at each other, I confused and wondering, he looking more defiant. Claude turned, walked to his dresser, and took a pair of socks from his drawer.

"Why?" I asked. "Why aren't you wearing your wedding ring?"

Claude refused to look at me. I watched as he sat on the edge of the bed and put his socks on, and then stood up, pulling on his trousers. Finally he spoke.

"It's not that I want a divorce," he said, his voice measured and terse, "but, in general, I am still very dissatisfied with the way you conduct yourself as a wife. I will not put my wedding ring on again until you are the kind of woman I want to be married to."

I felt as if a giant fist had been plunged down my throat. I could still see the list of needs Claude had handed me a few weeks before. Most of his requests, wanting the bathroom to himself in the morning, his dress shirts washed and ironed in the same day, and fifteen to twenty minutes on his own when he first got home from work, I felt willing to respect and accept. But his need to have sex with me much more frequently than I wanted to had become a sticking point between us. Although I knew that Claude's need for more intimacy was an attempt on his part to address the lack of love and connection he was feeling in relation to me, I was beginning to feel as if he were asking me to pour myself into a hole he had dug himself, setting me up to fail by asking me to heal a wound that could never heal.

Now, staring at Claude, I felt my body contract as I attempted to get a hold of the anger rising in me. I wanted to lunge at him, or else crumple to the floor and cry. But I could see, in Claude's eyes, that he was impervious to any response I might make. So, instead, I silently returned the ring to the top of his dresser and walked out of the room. I couldn't help wondering, as I made my way slowly down the stairs, how we could go for so long, feeling as if things were good and right between us, and then, in a blink of an eye, realize that what we shared was simply an idea. And no matter how frightening it was, I also knew, even if I hated to admit it, that regardless of what dreams I had had of my life or my marriage, Claude's life was his to live. I had no control over what he might or might not choose to do.

FOREIGN LANGUAGE

I TURNED THE ENVELOPE *over in my hands, looking for clues. It had arrived in our mailbox, wedged between an electric bill and a credit card offer from our bank. It was hand-written in a loopy, feminine scrawl, on lightweight airmail paper, and addressed to Claude Alan Martell. I didn't have to guess where it was from. Claude had returned not long ago from a ten-day business trip to Germany. And I was almost certain I knew something about the person who had sent it. Only a woman who had known intimacy with a man would have cared to know his middle name.*

Standing in the front hall, I carefully considered whether or not to open the envelope and read the letter inside. Although part of me didn't want to wait for Claude to come home and risk the possibility that he wouldn't tell me the truth about the envelope's contents, another, clearer part of me knew that my integrity meant even more to me now that I was holding evidence of the very real possibility that Claude had compromised his. I held the letter up to the light instead, but was unable to distinguish any words.

Something about Claude had felt foreign to me ever since his return. While I had been excited to see him, having experienced an increased sense of love and appreciation for him during the time he'd been away, Claude had seemed unusually distracted and vulnerable. When I had asked him, our first night together, about his time in Germany, his responses had been sketchy, elusive. He did admit that being away from me, our home, and family had given him a new perspective on his life, but he had also assured me that the shift he was feeling wasn't about anything that had happened in Germany.

Hearing his words, my heart had opened to him even more. I had held him in my arms for a long time, and then, tenderly, gently, we had made love. The next day, after work, Claude had pulled a box of cassette tapes out of his briefcase. It was an introductory course on how to speak German. "I want to learn how to speak another language" was his only explanation. I had accepted it, hoping it might mean we were one step closer to taking the vacation to Europe we'd sometimes talked about, oblivious to the possibility that his interest was due to something or someone else.

Now, walking as if in a trance up the stairs to our bedroom, going on vacation with Claude, no matter where it was, was the last thing I wanted to do. Now, more than ever, I needed to get away, to have some time and space on my own. Fortunately,

only two months before, as a Christmas gift, my sister Laura
had offered to watch my kids for ten days in July so I could finally go on my retreat. The timing, I realized now, couldn't
have been more perfect. Curling up into a tiny ball in the center of our bed, tears streaming down my cheeks, I willed my
body and my heart to hold on until then.

Unraveled

SATURDAY

THE MORNING SUN was streaming through the curtained windows when I woke. I stretched the length of my body and groaned contentedly, grateful to have slept late. Leaning back against a pile of pillows, I replayed my memories of the night before, of Roger's hands on my body, still feeling a visceral connection with him. Suddenly, my reverie was interrupted by a knock on the door.

"Just a minute," I called out, leaping out of bed and throwing on my robe.

Grinning, my heart thumping with anticipation, I pulled the door open. Roger was standing there, wearing a T-shirt, shorts, and running shoes, but when I saw the serious look on his face, I lost my grin.

"Is everything okay?" I asked, holding the door open wider. "Would you like to come in?"

Roger nodded his head, and stepped into the room. I

closed the door and turned to him. His posture was stiff, arms hanging at his side, fists clenched as if he was steeling himself for what he was about to say. His eyes, looking into mine, were cloudy with seriousness. My heart suddenly felt like a stone in my chest.

"I hardly slept last night. I need your help," he said, running his hands nervously from the top of his head down to his neck. He cleared his throat and continued. "Sometimes the greatest offering we can make to love is to say no. So what I need, what I think both our lives need, is for you to help me say no to what is happening between us."

The stone in my heart dropped with a thud into my gut. I searched his face for any sign of the joy we'd shared the night before, but it was not there. He was silent, looking now more determined than sad. I made no attempt to hide the hurt in my eyes. I felt chastised by him, and disappointed, but I also realized that part of me had been expecting this and probably even agreed.

I looked away, into the distance outside my window, and took a deep breath, attempting to loosen the band tightening around my chest. Even though every cell in my body was screaming "No," I turned back to him, tears in my eyes, and said, in a lifeless, you-can't-hurt-me voice that I recognized from my other life, "Yes. I will help you with what you asked."

I PRIED TWO RUSTY THUMBTACKS from the wall, and letting the screen door slam shut behind me, descended the porch steps, and walked back to where the path leading to the cabin turned off from the main trail. There I found a suitable tree and tacked two white index cards to it. The first read, "This way" with an arrow pointing in the direction of the cabin, the second, "Enter at your own risk," with a smiley face below. I wasn't sure if Roger had been to the cabin before, and since I knew in my heart he would come, I wanted to make it as easy as possible for him to find me.

Stepping back to admire my handiwork, I heard a rustle of leaves. I turned, smiling, expecting to see Roger, but instead a doe and her spotted fawn emerged into the late-morning light from the shadow of the trees. For a long, silent moment, the three of us stared at each other, and then, with a flick of their white tails, the deer disappeared into the woods.

As I strolled back to the cabin, I felt grateful for the way its sanctuary and the skittering, chattering, busyness of the forest had helped me regain the composure I'd lost two hours before. As soon as Roger had left my room, I had hurriedly packed a bag with some food, slipped a note under his door telling him I was going to the cabin, and ran, stumbling and crying through the woods. Blinded by tears and numb with disappointment, I hadn't even felt the sting of the thorns as they ripped through the skin on my bare ankles. Only later, sitting on the front porch of the cabin, had I noticed the rivulets of dry blood.

For an hour I had lain facedown on the bed in the cabin, sobbing into the pillows. I had felt as if the only part of my heart that hadn't broken after Hannah's death was now split in two. Roger's words had stung; I felt like a silly, childish schoolgirl for the secret wishes I had harbored, and grateful that what the two of us had shared last night hadn't developed into more. And yet, once my tears had dried, I had realized that something else was even more true; I wanted Roger to change his mind.

Now, returning to the cabin, I ate my lunch of fruit and cheese. I couldn't help thinking, as I stared out the window, watching the path, that Roger must by now be missing me terribly, and regretting what he had said. I felt certain that if his feelings were even half the intensity of mine, it wouldn't be long before he'd be making his way to me. After eating, I cleaned my dishes, filled one of the mugs with fresh flowers, and placed it in the center of the table. Looking around the room, I wondered where I should be when Roger arrived.

"Who am I fooling?" I said aloud. Like every one of

my favorite movies, I knew how the story was supposed to unfold. Climbing on top of the bed, I was careful not to muss the covers as I lay down and closed my eyes, just like Sleeping Beauty, certain that our happily-ever-after was assured.

I AWOKE TWO HOURS LATER, disoriented for a moment by my surroundings. As soon as I realized where I was, however, I jumped out of bed. Glancing around the cabin, I saw that everything was exactly as I had left it. Opening the door, I stepped onto the porch. A large blue jay, startled by my sudden appearance, cried out from his perch on a nearby branch and, flapping his wings, flew up and away. Walking quickly along the path, I saw in the distance the white of the index cards still tacked to the trees, but no sign of Roger. For a brief moment, I allowed myself to imagine he had either gotten a late start or was now hopelessly lost in the woods. But the sinking feeling in my stomach was telling another, much different story; Roger had clearly made his decision. He was not going to come.

Making my way back to the cabin, I sat, stunned, on the edge of the bed. Unlike the way I succumbed to the hysterical, all-consuming impulse that had inspired me to race to the cabin that morning, I knew I had to be absolutely certain of how I really felt and of what really mattered before deciding what to do. I willed myself to a quieter, more thoughtful task. With an unexpected sense of curiosity and calm, I began to turn my feelings over in my mind, fingering them and then setting them down, like stones on the beach.

At first glance, I felt hurt and rejected that Roger hadn't come, and certain it was somehow my fault. I had never in my life attempted to initiate something like this. I couldn't help thinking that my naïveté had contributed to what had happened. Perhaps he had been put off by the obvious hurt in my eyes that morning, or maybe the intensity of my feelings had scared him. I wished now that I had appeared less obvious, more independent, or braver. I felt silly and foolish for having opened myself so much to him, and wondered now if it had been a mistake.

And yet, even as the thought crossed my mind, I knew it wasn't true. I really *didn't* regret being so honest and open with him. I felt proud of the way I had conducted myself, and knew that everything I had said and done had come from a sense of clarity and confidence in me that I deeply trusted. I had never before felt so comfortable in my life, so beautiful and sure in my body. No matter what did or didn't happen with Roger, I didn't want anything to change that.

Standing up, I began to pace back and forth across the room. I felt charged, unusually restless, as if I were watching a crack in me slowly widening, seeing new aspects of myself being revealed. The most shocking, almost too surprising even to admit, was that I did not feel ashamed of my behavior, of my wish to be with a man other than my husband. I had always prided myself on being a good, moral, upstanding person. I felt nothing like the kind of bold, uncaring, irresponsible woman I imagined committed adultery. Adultery, I had always believed, was a sin against God.

Snippets of every lecture my father had given me as a young girl about the evils of premarital sex, and Claude's previous accusations, however unfounded then, whispered now in my ear. All my life, those voices had asked, cajoled, and demanded that I damp down any part of myself that might be expressed erotically. And because I had believed I had to be "good" in order to be loved, I had obeyed. This morning, I now realized, had been no exception. I had come to the cabin not because I wanted to be there, but because I thought Roger had wanted me to. I had believed he simply needed time and space away from me to think things through, and my fantasy was that because I had been so obedient, he would "reward" me by coming.

Sitting down on the edge of the bed, I stared out the

window at the empty path. Years of frustration and anger began to well up in my gut, and for the first time in my life, I also felt the overwhelming sense of powerlessness underneath. It was as if I had been waiting on the edge of that bed forever, believing that someone else would have to do something or something else would have to happen before my "real" life could begin. Like a barometer, I had allowed my actions to be dictated by the wants and needs of others, secretly hoping that if I were good enough and patient enough, something good would happen. I was always on the cusp of something bigger and better. The held breath of "any moment now" was as familiar to me as the pause of my heart between beats.

Closing my eyes, I inhaled a long, slow breath, and felt my heart soften as I inched closer to its deepest secret. What if I had gotten it all wrong, if all these years I had completely missed the point of my life? What if it didn't have anything to do with waiting, with trying to be good? My eyes flew open. There was such a sense of clarity and purity in this realization that I knew that it was true. This room, this body, and these feelings right here, right now, *were* my life. Whether good or bad, perfect or imperfect, what mattered wasn't about what happened outside myself or whether others approved; what mattered was how fully and unapologetically I was able to be who I was.

Staring into nothing, I felt my heart beating in my chest, my breath drawing in and out of my lungs, and every inch of my body tingling with sensation. I had lived so much of my life feeling under the thumb of someone else—first my parents and then Claude—that it had taken me until now to realize that regardless of what other people thought about what I should or shouldn't do, it was I who got to choose! I knew then that the most beautiful and vibrant part of myself was this creative, sexual, life-affirming aliveness, which I believed could come only from God. I could feel it calling me into a new kind of courage in my life, and even if others, including Roger, felt threatened or overwhelmed by it, I needed to trust it more and more.

Slowly, calmly, I stood up, finally knowing what I needed to do. Packing the remains of my lunch in my bag, turning off the light, and closing the door, I set off on the path toward the retreat center, knowing that what my life was wanting had nothing to do with whether or not Roger and I would ever make love. Without needing or even caring to know what might happen as a result, I simply knew that I could no longer say no to what was happening. Roger was free to make his own decision. But I had to say "yes."

I TAPPED LIGHTLY on his door and heard him call for me to come in. He was seated in front of his computer, in the soft light of the afternoon sun, wearing only his running shorts. As he turned to look at me, he was not smiling. Neither was I. But my body felt strong and tall, my feet were firmly planted, and I knew I could deeply trust what I was about to do.

"I thought you went to the cabin," Roger said, standing and moving toward me, his lips pressed tightly together. From the tone of his voice I could tell he was exasperated.

"I did," I said, not moving. I took a deep breath, feeling carefully for the right words. "I came back because the more I thought about it, the more I realized that I was there not because I wanted to be, but because I thought *you* wanted me to be."

Roger cocked his head, and studied my face. I took another deep breath and forged ahead.

"I'm sorry I interrupted you. I know you're busy. I just had to tell you one thing." I paused.

"This morning you asked me to help you say no to what is happening." I stopped as my voice faltered and tears began to well up in my eyes. I swallowed and cleared my throat, willing myself not to cry. Roger seemed frozen in place. Our eyes were locked. My heart felt full, my body now still.

"I cannot help you with what you asked," I said.

For a long moment, neither of us moved, my words resonating in the space between us. Finally Roger spoke.

"What do you mean?" he asked softly, but the tone of his voice had shifted and was now gentler, softer, measured, suggesting he already knew. Looking into his eyes, I felt the ground under my feet and the clarity in my heart.

"I am not afraid," I said, buoyed by the calm within me. "I deeply trust what is happening right now, in me and in my life. I have room for you to do whatever is best for you, for you to say no if you need to. But I have to say yes—yes to my life, yes to this, yes to whatever is happening between us."

As the last word dropped from my lips, I felt a wave of emotion welling up in me. Tears began to slide down my cheeks, not from sadness or uncertainty, but from relief. I felt chastened, cleansed of all my previous shortcomings and sins. I knew that, other than the moment of my children's births and Hannah's death, I had never been so close to God.

Roger was no longer immobile. Stepping into the space between us, he opened his arms, and wrapped them around me. As my body softened into his embrace and I inhaled the scent of his bare skin, the story of my afternoon at the cabin began to pour out of me. I told him everything, the history of my regrets, my disappointments at not having had more courage, the way I knew I could no longer say no to the most beautiful and true parts of me, that I could no longer worry about doing the "right thing."

While I spoke, Roger listened, nodding his head thoughtfully, his eyes urging me on. At one point, he left me briefly to get a washcloth from the bathroom, which he used to dry my tears and clean the dripping mascara off my cheeks. I was so full of the story I was telling, I hardly registered Roger's actions as I watched him brush his teeth, and splash cologne on his neck; then, his hand pressed firmly against the small of my back, he gently guided me ahead of him up the stairs.

Not until we were sitting side by side on the edge of his bed did I return to my body and register where I was. I fell silent then and, glancing around his room, noticed his clothes thrown over the backs of chairs, a few candles and a stick of incense burning, the rumpled sheets on his unmade bed. I turned to look at Roger. The light in his eyes was as soft as moonlight as he lay back, pulling me toward him, until we were lying, like spoons, across his bed. I felt the strength and aliveness in his body along the full length of mine. For a long time, the two of us lay there, breathing as one breath, inhaling the peace that had descended between us.

Unraveled

Finally, slowly, I rolled my body over, toward him. Our faces were almost touching. I studied the lines in the corners of his eyes, the light stubble of beard on his cheek, and traced, with my finger, the bow of his lips.

"You see," I whispered, smiling at him, "this is all I needed. This, right here, is enough," I said.

He smiled. Then, ever so gently, he touched his lips softly, then more firmly, against mine. Returning his kisses, my body began to melt, pressing against his. Pausing, Roger pulled his face away, his eyes dancing.

"I thought you said that holding each other was enough," he chided me, playfully.

"It was," I said, lightly kissing the top of his nose. "But this is much better." Laughing and wrapping our arms around each other, our lips came together, this time hungrily. Then the real embrace began.

HOLLOW TRUTH

THE LAMP ON WILL'S *bedside table cast its soft light across the pages of* Farmer Boy, *by Laura Ingalls Wilder, the nighttime book Will and I had been reading. Will was beside me on the bed, his eyes slowly closing. I loved the feeling of his warm, soft form next to mine. Although he was now ten years old, there remained a sweetness and innocence in him that I treasured, as well as a maturity that threatened to break my heart.*

Watching him play basketball with his friends, listening to him tell me about a video game's complicated moves, or over-hearing him share a story about Hannah with his sisters, I felt a sense of pride and respect for the young man he was becom-ing. Wrapping my arms around him, I held him close as I lay quietly with his head nestled into the space between my shoul-der and chin.

"I love you, Mom," he said.

"I love you, too, Muffin," I said, kissing him again, this

time twice on each cheek. "*I think it's time to say good night.*" *Will smiled at me sleepily and held his floppy blue bunny up to my face.*

"*Don't forget, Mom, Bunny needs a kiss too.*" *I smiled and dropped a kiss on the tip of the bunny's nose. Will grinned, readjusted the bunny beside him under the blankets, then rolled over onto his side.*

"*Mom,*" *he asked in a quiet voice, as I reached for the light switch,* "*are you and Dad going to get a divorce?*"

My arm froze in midair. Lately, despite the fact that Claude and I had returned to marriage counseling, there was no hiding from our kids the difficulty we were having. Although Claude, when confronted by me, had insisted he and the German woman who sent him the letter had dated and kissed but not had sex, I found it difficult to accept even the idea that Claude had considered being with someone else, outside of our marriage. Ironically, I had spent years reassuring him that I would never commit adultery, because he had so frequently insisted I was going to leave him for another man. Despite the therapist's help, the arguments between us were as loud and ugly as ever, the intensity and consistency of our anger toward each other matched only by the frustration we both seemed to feel.

Now, looking into Will's eyes, I knew his question was understandable, even inevitable, but because of the quiet of the house and the simplicity of the moment, it had caught me off guard. Taking a deep breath, I prayed for the right words, and tried to imagine how uncertain and confused he must feel. It hadn't been that long ago when he had wrapped his arms around our legs as the three of us danced together. He was probably wondering why the pendulum between his parents seemed to swing so far from one side to the other. But as I struggled to find the words to reassure his questioning heart, I felt strangled by my own uncertainty and questions. How could I ever explain to Will what I could not even understand myself?

I knew that, despite our difficulties, I felt a sense of love for Claude that, though elusive and painful, was deep and necessary, too. The mystery of why we were together had been answered at the moment of Hannah's death and at each of our four children's births. If it weren't for our children, I was certain that we would not be together, but because of them, we wanted to understand why our being together could feel both right and wrong, at the same time.

Reaching for Will, I gathered him into my arms again and gave him another, bigger hug.

"I'm sorry for how painful and confusing all of this must feel to you, Will," I said, trying not to cry. "Even I don't understand why Dad and I are having so much trouble. But the one thing I know is that, even though we don't do it very well, we do love each other. And more than anything else, we definitely love each of you kids. What I can promise you is that Dad and I are doing everything we can to work things out. Neither of us wants to get a divorce."

Unraveled

I felt Will's body relax in my arms, as I continued to hold him.

"Thanks, Mom. That's what I needed to hear," Will said, finally, wiping his eyes and laying back down. Kissing him once more and then turning off the light, I appreciated that Will seemed relieved by my answer, but I couldn't ignore the way my words echoed hollowly in my head.

REALITY, INTERRUPTED

THE OTHER MOTHERS AND I could barely hear each other speak over the noise our children were making. Sitting next to my friend Elizabeth, I sighed, exasperated that it was taking me so long to get to the end of the story I was telling. Constantly interrupted by one child or another, we had started and stopped our conversation in the middle of a sentence too many times to count.

My life, it seemed, had become a stream of interruptions. I could barely complete a thought. Whether it was the phone ringing, the clothes dryer buzzing, or some question only I could answer, my attention was constantly being redirected from what I was doing to what someone else wanted me to do. This morning it had taken me two and a half hours to get Will off to school and Margaret and Madelaine dressed and fed, and five minutes before we were supposed to leave for play group, the girls were ready, but I hadn't yet brushed my teeth or changed out of my pajamas. I wasn't proud, either, of the way

I had begun to express my frustration. More than once in the past month, I had stood in front of Claude or one of my kids, screaming, "Leave me alone" at the top of my lungs.

Many of the bereaved moms I knew had spent weeks after their child's death refusing to get out of bed or hiding in the bottom of a dark closet. My life hadn't afforded the same possibility to me, and because of that, I felt that my children had suffered more than they needed to due to my shortcomings and exhaustion as a bereaved mother. I was anxious to go on my retreat, in order to rest and figure out what needed to happen next. I also longed for even simpler comforts—being able to sleep late, not having to worry about making a meal, or about picking up after anyone else. Life without Hannah would be bearable only if I were able to integrate what she had taught me about being honest, about what mattered, and if I were able to be the mother my children needed and deserved.

Interrupting my reverie, Elizabeth caught my eye.

"If you could be granted one wish right now, what would it be?" she asked. I closed my eyes briefly, and immediately saw myself lying in the blazing sun on a deserted white sand beach, a gentle breeze blowing in off a sapphire blue sea.

"A week of solitude on a remote Caribbean island," I said.

Elizabeth laughed out loud. "Oh, Maria, you are so funny," she giggled.

"Why? What would you wish for?" I asked, sensing I had once again missed part of the conversation.

"Oh, that's easy." Elizabeth wasn't laughing now. "I'd wish for a lifetime of happiness for each of my kids."

I smiled through my teeth, but said "fuck, fuck, fuck" under my breath. I, of all people, should know better by now. I was sick and tired of getting questions like that one wrong.

Unraveled

A NEW LEAF

THE AIR WAS COOL, *but the dark soil, warmed by the sun, felt good in my hands. I had not realized until now that a soil's richness can be determined not only by its color but also by its heft and weight, the pungency of its scent, and the ease with which it parts to let a plant's roots in. For years, the idea of planting a garden had been turning over in my mind. Like painting, though, I had imagined that it required lots of understanding and skill, and therefore was something I would only be able to do when I had more time. But lately, feeling disconnected from life and restless, I had spent hours looking out the window, watching crocuses push their heads aboveground and the trees unfurling their new leaves. I had decided I needed something new to occupy my thoughts, and planting a garden seemed the right thing.*

Now, poking little pockets into the earth with my fingers, and dropping in pearls of seeds, I felt grateful to be doing something so hands-on and productive. I could already imagine myself in the summer, filling vases with my own fresh flowers, watching my kids pull new carrots from the earth and snap ripe tomatoes from their stems. One of my favorite aspects of this garden had nothing to do with its flowers, herbs, and vegetables, though. A secret path of flat stones wove in and out through the plantings, leading to a tiny stone angel and birdbath in the middle, a simple memorial to Hannah.

Standing up, bending the tension out of my back, I smiled at Margaret and Madelaine, who, with their sand shovels, had dug their own hole, big enough for a small tree, in one corner of the garden, and were now filling it with packets of leftover seeds and handfuls of grass and twigs. The two of them, now two and three years old, were rarely separated. Though they were sixteen months apart, many people automatically assumed they were twins, not necessarily because they looked alike but because their delight in being together was obvious, and the connection between them so unique.

"Hey, you two," I called out from my side of the garden, "How's it going over there?"

"Good, Mommy," Margaret said, as Madelaine, at the sound of my voice, stood up and began waving her shovel in my direction. "Come see. Me and Maddy are making some garden soup."

Smiling, I made my way toward them. Both girls were now squatting beside the edge of the huge hole they had dug. "Here, Maddy," Margaret said, handing Madelaine an enormous stick. "You're the littlest so you can stir first."

The whole scene unfolded in my mind seconds before it actually happened. Before I could stop her, Madelaine reached both hands toward Margaret and took the stick from her. Because Madelaine was already squatting and leaning too close to the edge of the hole, the weight of the stick tipped the balance. Margaret and I watched helplessly as Madelaine tumbled into the bed of grass, leaves, and twigs at the bottom of the hole.

"Don't worry, Maddy, I'll save you," Margaret shouted, scrambling to a standing position and jumping feet first, as if off a diving board, into the pit with Madelaine.

"Oh, my goodness," I said, finally reaching them and leaning over to lift them out. "Are you two okay?" I need not have asked; their smiling, dirt-streaked faces and giggles told me what I needed to know. Checking them quickly to make sure there weren't any unreported injuries, I wrapped the two of them in my arms.

"I think this is a good time to take a break and have some lunch. What do you two think?" I asked.

"Yes!" they both shouted, clapping their hands. "But, Mommy," Margaret said, trying to look serious, "I hope you're not going to give us soup."

Laughing, I scooped the two of them up and carried the giggling bundle of little-girl silliness into the house. Glancing out the kitchen window while I prepared lunch a few minutes later, I smiled at the garden with its neat rows of plantings, Hannah's stone angel, and the girls' garden-soup hole at one end. I realized then that the real magic of gardening wasn't contained in any of the books that lined library and bookstore shelves. While it was true that to garden was to establish a relationship with the turning of the earth, the waxing and waning of the moon, and the subtle shifts between seasons, what mattered even more to me was that the connection between my life and the earth was richer and more joyful for having shared it with my girls.

Unraveled

SUNDAY

I WOKE SLOWLY, feeling dazed and dreamy, in my own bed. My body felt full, as if the love Roger and I had shared was still resonating through me. A breath of warmth wafted into my nostrils as I lifted the sheet. Slowly, gratefully, I inhaled the mossy, musky scent of him, lingering on my skin. Closing my eyes, I ran my hands up and down my body, recalling the touch of his fingers as I drifted through my memories of the night before.

Soft, moist mouths, bellies rising and falling, swollen, oozing, trembling, I had felt my heart, petal by petal, gently opening. I had been both in my body and outside it as he entered me, as we stared into each other, eyes wide open. "We are there," he had whispered, his eyes filling with tears. Later, he had gradually unwound his body from our embrace and, kneeling at the foot of the bed, pressed his hands together in a posture of prayer, then lifted and kissed my feet.

I had felt nothing awkward, uncertain, or shameful in that place. Fully awake to myself, aware of every movement in my body, I had surrendered everything—all my regrets, pain, faults, and unlived dreams—and felt the self-imposed boundaries that had defined who I was and wasn't all these years, like the sides of a box, fall away. Time was elastic and also compressed, as I, without shame or regret, felt myself and allowed myself to be seen truly naked. Even now, in the light of the morning after, the place where he had entered me still numb from his fullness, I knew that in that moment of ultimate vulnerability, I had become both his and mine.

Rising slowly from the bed, I felt a new awareness in my body. Every movement, even reaching for the glass of water on the table beside me, felt deliberate and measured. Standing in the shower, I inhaled the soap's lavender scent and felt my muscles softening as the warm water coursed over my body. Toweling myself off, I stared at the image of my face in the mirror, half expecting to see some other, more experienced, knowing woman there, relieved to see that the eyes looking into mine were the ones I had always seen.

Once dressed, I went downstairs to the kitchen, opened the door, and stepped outside. The light, the birds, and the waves of grass—everything was sharper to my eye. Walking through the meadow to the end of the path, I realized why everything looked different to me now. For the first time in my life, I knew that Love was not something exclusive or attached to one person or idea. It was the experience of being wholly and completely one's Self, without boundaries or hesitation. And in that, because of that, everything and everyone else could be truly seen.

I HAD JUST RETURNED to my room and opened my journal, when I heard a knock on my door. Opening it, I saw Roger standing there, all smiles and blowing me kisses, still sweaty from his morning run.

"Good morning," he said, bouncing excitedly from one foot to the other. "What were you planning to do on this perfectly lovely day?"

"I was thinking of taking a long walk to Thoreau, the cabin in the woods," I said, smiling. "Although it *is* my own secret hideaway, I'd love to share it with you."

"I'd like that very much," he said, his eyes twinkling mischievously. "As you know, I've not been there before."

Laughing, I nodded "yes" as he playfully grabbed me around my waist and lifted me off the floor, twirling me in circles as if we were ice-dancing partners. Throwing my head back, relaxing in his arms, I felt positively delicate in my long, tall body. Lowering me to the floor, he grabbed my shoulders and pulled me close for a long kiss.

"Good. That's settled then," he said, breaking away. "I'm going to take a quick shower. Let's meet in half an hour in my room."

I returned my journal to the desk drawer, picked up my backpack, and went down to the kitchen to make sandwiches for our lunch. Returning up the two flights of stairs to Roger's room, I knocked on the door, and then entered. I could hear the shower running in the bathroom. I set my backpack on the sofa, and then wandered around the room, looking more closely at Roger's life, at Roger's things.

I tried to imagine what it might be like for us to live together—waking to his embrace, listening to the sound of him getting ready in the bathroom each morning, seeing our clothes tumbled together in the laundry basket at the foot of the bed. I realized that I couldn't quite imagine any of it actually happening—not so much because I didn't think it would or could, but because I was now so engaged and interested in my own life, that I had no need to imagine a life more alive and real than this one I was just getting to know.

Unraveled

I LAY IN ROGER'S ARMS on the cabin's twin bed, watching the afternoon shadows move along the wall, listening to the frogs calling from the pond down the hill and the sound of Roger's breath while he slept. Roger had loved everything about the tiny space, just as I had known he would. Seeing his genuine enthusiasm for a place I loved so much, I was reminded that the connection between us wasn't based on where and how we had lived; the two of us shared similar perspectives about what mattered and spoke the language of a world that, until now, I had thought was mine alone.

The two of us had arrived just after noon, in time to eat lunch on the steps of the front porch. At one point during our meal, a beautiful blue dragonfly had landed on the edge of Roger's plate.

"Oh, look," Roger had exclaimed in a hushed voice. The two of us had marveled at the insect's oily iridescence, his long tail twitching, and his filmy, see-through wings fluttering in the breeze. "Dragonflies were my first introduction to beauty," Roger said quietly. "I still remember when I saw one for the first time. I must have been three or four."

Looking at Roger while he spoke, I could almost imagine what he must have looked like then. He would have had more hair, of course, perhaps a tumble of blond curls, the same light blue eyes and thick, strong legs. No doubt his mother had had her hands full following him around as he explored the world, picking up everything and looking at it closely, before dropping it and scampering to the next thing.

After lunch, I had taken him on a short tour in and around the cabin, refilled the mug on the table with more fresh flowers, and then the two of us had fallen into bed. Now, careful not to disturb him, I disentangled myself from his sleepy embrace. Slipping my feet into my sandals, I opened the screen door, stepped through, and then eased it closed. The air was hushed and humid. Tiny bugs buzzed around my head and face as I followed the path from the cabin to the main trail. Picking my way carefully through the leaves and prickly branches, I paused every once in a while to wipe drops of sweat from my brow.

Ahead, through the trees, I saw the reason for my foray. The once white index cards, now wind-whipped and faded, were still tacked to the trees. I had noticed them earlier, as Roger and I passed, but had decided then not to retrieve them. This, I knew, was necessarily a solitary task. Approaching now, I saw that the ink on them had smeared into unintelligible blue markings and then, in the warmth of the sun, dried. Removing the tacks, then the cards from the tree, I put the tacks in the pocket of my shorts, then ripped the cards into tiny pieces and put them in my pockets too.

Unraveled

Walking slowly back toward the cabin, I slipped my hands into my pockets and fingered the pieces of paper there. They seemed to me now so many pieces of un- lived dreams no longer needed. I was already lifetimes away from those hours spent in loneliness and longing just a day before.

Maria Housden

PEEKING BEHIND THE CURTAIN

I WAS CURLED UP in the wing chair next to the fireplace in our living room, lost in a book about reincarnation, while a thin ribbon of smoke from a stick of incense filled the air with its lavender scent. In the distance, as if from another world, I could hear the thump, thump, thump of Will and his friends dribbling a basketball in the driveway outside, and Margaret and Madelaine giggling as they played with Barbie dolls in their room upstairs. Although Claude was due home any minute from work, and the whole house was strewn with toys, pieces of board games abandoned halfway through, and the remains of the girls' picnic lunch, I was too engrossed in my book to feel concerned.

These days, I wasn't waiting for the answers to come to me; I was doing everything I could to get God's attention.

A small group of friends and I had recently started meeting at my house on Friday mornings to read and discuss books on topics ranging from dream interpretation to psychic phenomena to the inherent wisdom of other spiritual traditions. While my orientation to God and life had always felt particularly Christian, I also was instinctively drawn to the more mystical aspects of other religions. The idea of reincarnation, for example, particularly appealed to me, not only because it offered a reason and context for Hannah's life and death that was comforting and made sense, but also because I had sometimes felt an otherwise unexplainable relationship with other people and times that the understanding of reincarnation validated for me.

Friday Morning Spiritual Group, as we called it, offered me an opportunity to converse with a community of similarly curious women who, like me, were living mostly conventional lives as wives and at-home moms. Where I had once met with friends to drink coffee and talk about our relationships and kids, I was now drinking coffee and talking about God and the nature of reality. I was feeling less and less like a weirdo trying to fit into a more traditional world, and more like the young woman I had once been who frequently wandered into other people's churches in the middle of the week to light a candle, sit in silence, and pray.

Hearing the sound of Claude's heavy footfalls on the steps, I lifted my head. As he picked his way through the debris strewn across the living room and came to a stop in front of me, my eyes, having been focused so long on the printed page, took a moment to refocus.

"What's for dinner," Claude said, his face darkening.

"I don't know yet," I said, "I got lost in this great book I'm reading."

Claude glanced at the title, Many Lives, Many Masters.

"You're crazy," he said, disgusted. "All this hocus-pocus incense and reincarnation shit. I'm sick of all those crazy friends of yours hanging out here too." Turning on his heel, he stomped up the steps to our room. Closing the book, I smiled.

These days, feeling more confident and sure of who I was becoming, I no longer felt the sting of Claude's criticism in the same way. I understood that his biting words and resentment of the friendships and interests I was developing outside my relationship with him was a symptom of his need to keep me close to home. And I refused to allow his threats or anger clip my wings.

OCEAN OF LOVE

THE SUN WAS WARM on my face as I watched Will body-surf on the waves of the incoming tide while Margaret poked tattered seagull feathers into the turrets of a sand castle, and Madelaine buried my feet in the sand. The beach was deserted except for the four of us and an elderly man who was trolling for treasure with a metal detector held in both hands. I loved coming to the ocean. The endless horizon and the sound of the waves never failed to open me to a bigger perspective on my life, and there was something wild and precise about the slope of dunes whose dips and crests had been cut into the sand by fierce winds.

Smiling at Madelaine, I began to wiggle my toes underneath the mound she had just built. She and I started giggling as soon as the tips of my toes broke through. Quickly, she dumped small handfuls of sand on top of my feet.

"Come here, Margaret," she called out above the sound of the waves, "Mommy's feet are trying to get away!"

Margaret jumped up, grinning, and started running toward

us. "Don't worry, Maddy, I'm coming," she said. Dropping onto the sand next to Madelaine, the two of them began scooping mounds on top of my legs. Now all three of us were laughing, as no matter how much sand they piled on top of me, my toes kept wiggling through. Will, catching a glimpse of the commotion, splashed his way out of the water.

"Help us, Willy," Margaret and Madelaine called out in unison. Will, glancing at me to make sure it was okay, lay down on the sand. Digging his feet in, he used his arms like the jaws of a front loader and shoved a giant mound of sand onto my feet, completely burying the girls' feet, too.

"Grrr," I growled, grabbing at Margaret and Madelaine, who squealed and landed in my arms. Not wanting to leave Will out, I heaved my legs out of the sand and, like scissors, trapped him too. The four of us fell into each other, laughing. Breathless and beaming, I gradually extracted myself from the pile and gave each of them a kiss.

Watching them play together, I realized that as a mother, I always had loved my children unconditionally, but as a wife, I still longed for a deeper, more trusting intimacy than I had known with Claude. Staring past the ocean's horizon, I knew that, as far as my marriage was concerned, I had been hanging on too long to the edge of a sinking boat. But beneath that knowing, I was harboring an unspoken fear. What if the problems between Claude and me were more mine than his, and I was incapable of being in a healthy relationship with a man?

MONDAY

FOR THE FIRST TIME since I had arrived, I opened the door to my minivan and climbed in. I had decided, on waking, that I would head into town to buy a good-bye card for Roger and a copy of his most recently published book, since I was scheduled to leave early the next morning, to drive to my sister's house to pick up my kids. I also suspected it might be good for me to venture for a short time into the outside world, not unlike an astronaut who has to reacclimate to earth's oxygenated air before attempting reentry.

Turning the key in the ignition, I glanced around at the Happy Meal toys, box of baby wipes, and Nintendo magazines littering the floor. Sniffing the air, I detected a not-so-familiar odor that I quickly realized was coming from a crumpled-up fast-food bag one of the kids had stuffed under a backseat. I left the engine running and carried the bag with its offending odor to a garbage can outside the barn. The poignancy of the moment didn't escape me; after a week of freshly grown produce from the garden, I wanted nothing to do with fast food.

Climbing back into the minivan, I smiled at the tumble of toys and books, savoring the realization that tomorrow I would be able to see and hold my kids. No matter how much the time away had nourished me, I also knew that being separated from them for so long had been bearable only because I truly believed it would enable me to be a more patient, trusting, and joyful mother, and I now felt more certain than ever that I would not allow the toxicity of Claude's and my unhappiness with our lives and each other to contaminate our family any longer.

Easing the car out onto the road, I drove along the highway much more slowly than usual, content to stay in the right lane while others raced past. I knew that my decreased appetite for speed and fast food was only a taste of what lay ahead. Without question, Claude's dream of returning to the way things had been before Hannah got sick was something I could not share. I had seen too much about what else was possible, for me and for my life. Though Claude had taken the first step by refusing to wear his wedding ring, it was I who would have to make the final break, to reconstellate the whole of my life in order to bring this same sense of love and possibility to my kids.

Unraveled

~~~∂

IN THE FLICKERING CANDLELIGHT, I ran my
fingers along the dips and curves of Roger's body and
along the ridge of a scar on his hip. I inhaled the scent of
him deep into my lungs and prayed that his gaze might
be imprinted forever in the darkness behind my eyes.
The whisper of hope that we might see each other again
was weighed down with the more real possibility that we
wouldn't. Our love, though, seemed bigger than any uncertainty about what might or might not happen; its
blessing, an unspeakable promise.

Earlier, the two of us had shared our last evening
meal at an Italian restaurant in town. After four glasses of
chilled Pinot Grigio between us, as the waiter brought
baskets of bread, plates of salad and pasta, coffee, and dessert, Roger and I had alternated between gazing deeply
into each other's eyes and doubling over with laughter as
Roger began saying everything with a ridiculously exaggerated, thick, Italian accent.

I felt like the luckiest woman in the world, knowing
I had loved and was still loving such a good and handsome man. Being with him, I felt like a more beautiful
version of myself, and grateful too that, while packing
for my retreat, I had added at the last minute my favorite
turquoise-colored summer dress, a pair of dangly pearl
earrings, and black, strappy sandals. At the end of our

meal, while we waited for the waiter to prepare the bill, I had pulled a copy of Roger's book *Sacred Journeys in a Modern World* from my purse and shyly handed it to him.

"I'd love for you to inscribe it," I said. Roger had taken the book from me, perched his eyeglasses on the end of his nose, and removed his pen from his eyeglass case. Staring thoughtfully into space for a long moment, he then turned toward me and said, "If you don't mind, I'd like to keep this for a while and give my inscription some thought. Under the circumstances, I want it to be true and circumspect, at the same time."

Now, savoring the warmth and solidity of Roger's embrace, in the flickering light of his room, I felt more aware than ever of the incredible, impossible circum-stance we were in. Although it seemed crazy, it also felt right that there had been no talk of exchanging addresses or phone numbers, and, as far as I knew, neither of us expected to either. As much as I loved and appreciated this time we had together, for almost sixteen years I had been a satellite, orbiting around one man; the last thing I wanted was to leave one constellation to orbit around another.

Instead, I felt certain that it was time for me to create a new container for the simpler, more creative, and less angry life I knew I wanted to share with my kids. And I also trusted that, once we had settled into this new life I was about to create, I might consider touching in again with Roger. After all, I had learned enough in the past ten days not to leave everything to the fates; I had seen his e-mail address earlier in the week and was sure it was one I'd remember.

PEELING THE SKIN OFF A
SNAKE

I SAT IN THE DARK of the quiet house, staring at the blank page in front of me. For almost a month, I had been try- ing to begin the book I wanted to write about Hannah and her life, believing it might be the answer to the restlessness I was feeling. But after days of working and pages and pages of words, I had managed to get only three days of the story down. Sitting at the dining room table now, I realized that, however much I wanted to write it, I couldn't. It wasn't time.

Instead, I pulled my journal in front of me and began to pour all the words I dared not say aloud to Claude or anyone else onto the page. My life had always seemed more under- standable, more manageable, when I was able to articulate my feelings in writing. Even so, as I reread the words I had just written in my journal and stared at the moon through the win- dow, searching for more, I knew that writing and publishing a book would have to happen in some other life than the one I was living. My time and attention were already so stretched by my responsibilities as a wife and mother, the idea of my writing and publishing a book or even going back to work seemed an impossible thing.

Any hope I felt for my future now came from knowing that the ten-day retreat my sister had arranged for me was on the horizon. I was scheduled to drive to Michigan with my kids in early July, less than a month from now. Already, it was feeling as if a door that had been opened for me, just ahead, and in no time at all, I would know what was on the other side. Until then, I was simply clinging to the coattails of God.

Closing my journal, I stood up from the dining room table and carried my mug of now cooled tea into the kitchen, rinsed it out, and laid it on the top shelf of the dishwasher. The last of the embers had almost burned down in the fireplace, as I walked through the downstairs, making sure windows were closed and doors were locked. Pausing in front of the refrigerator, I stared for a moment at the finger paintings Margaret and Madelaine had made in preschool. In one, a painting of our family, Claude, Will, Margaret, Madelaine, and I were smiling and holding hands, while Hannah, as an angel with a sparkly halo, hovered above us.

Before turning off the last living room light, I caught a glimpse of my reflection in the picture window. It was as if I were suddenly on the outside of my self and my life, looking in. I saw my face, tired but young, my tall, thin form, surrounded by the furnishings and accouterments of a comfortable life. I suddenly felt ashamed to feel so ungrateful and restless in a story that so many others, even I from the outside looking in, could see was a blessed thing. Climbing the steps to the kids' rooms, I stood for a while in each doorway, watching them sleep. Their faces were so peaceful in the moonlight. Whatever hell Claude and I had been putting them through, there was no sign of it now. Perhaps it still wasn't too late for them, for us, to find another way to make things work.

Sliding into bed, beside Claude's sleeping form, I realized that by pouring so much time and attention into trying to figure out what I was supposed to be doing with my life, I'd been peeling the skin off the snake, rather than waiting for it to shed itself. I understood now that the real challenge facing me wasn't about willing myself into another life, but rather being grateful for the life I already had.

Unraveled

A MAN HOLDING ON TO A WOMAN LETTING GO

THE SUN WAS MELTING behind the hills into pools of gold and orange. I switched the car's headlights on and reached for the cell phone. Not knowing whether the retreat center where I would be staying for the next ten days had a phone or not, I decided to check in with Claude while I could. My heart raced with anticipation as I listened to the ring of the phone in my ear and prayed he would answer. The two of us hadn't spoken since our strained good-byes in the driveway a few days before, but my body had already forgotten about the hurt between us. I couldn't wait to tell Claude that despite the difficulties we'd experienced in our marriage in the past years, I had not forgotten how much I still loved him.

"Hello," Claude answered.

"Hello, Claude. It's me," I said, my heart leaping in my chest.

"Oh, I'm so glad you called," he replied quietly. "I've

been thinking about a lot since you left, and there's something
I need to say."

I smiled, imagining that this was the scene in the movie of
my life where everything was going to be made right. The pain
we had been tossing back and forth was about to melt away.
Claude was going to tell me he loved me and missed me and
would do anything if I would only hurry home. And I would
tell him I loved him too, and that because of the strength of our
love, everything was possible between us.

Claude was silent on the other end of the phone. I realized
I was holding my breath.

"First, I really want our marriage to work. I'm willing to
compromise on everything we've discussed with the marriage
counselor except I do need to have more sex. The other thing,"
he continued, "is that I found your journals and I've been
reading them. There are a few entries I want to read out loud
to you now, and when I'm finished, I want you to explain
why you wrote what you did."

There was a crackling noise on the line, as the connection
began to break up. I heard Claude's voice as he began to read my
own words to me. I pictured my journals where I had left them,
safely tucked away in my underwear drawer, and remembered
the pain I had poured onto their pages. Claude's voice droned
on, but I made out less and less of what he was saying as the
static on the line became louder and more disruptive. My fingers
gripped the steering wheel. I felt my breath rising and falling in

my chest. I was aware of the beating of my heart and was surprised by how measured and calm it was.

I knew that any other time in my life I would have felt a thousand other things in a moment like this—outrage, violation, shock, despair—but instead, untouched by Claude's words or actions, I felt nothing but a deep sense of love and compassion for him.

A certainty—strong and separate from this man and his needs—began to pour through me. I finally understood, in the quietest place inside, that no matter how much I loved Claude, I could no longer feel responsible for his happiness, just as I could not make him responsible for mine. Happiness, contentment, and love were not experiences we could give each other; they were simply experiences we could share or be. I had been toting a bubble of compromises, sacrifices, and submission around with me the whole of our relationship, believing that if I were to try harder, be more loving, do more, both of us would finally be happy. And in this single moment it had released its hold and, like a balloon, floated up and away from me.

Whatever was going to happen in the days ahead, I knew I was now a million miles away, and I was never going back.

TUESDAY

THE WOODS WERE ALMOST SILENT as I made my way toward the cabin in the early-morning light, stopping and bending down now and then to pick handfuls of tiny purple and yellow flowers that lined the path. I had decided, on waking, to spend the first few hours of my last day rocking on Thoreau's front porch. It seemed necessary that I return one last time to the place where my life had awakened to itself, especially since it was likely that I might never see it again.

Rounding the bend, I saw the rosy glow of the dawn spread like a baby's blanket in the sky beyond the trees and the edge of the cabin's pitched roof. A chubby brown woodchuck was nosing his way through clumps of grass in the front yard, while several jays, perched on surrounding branches, warned each other of my unannounced arrival. My pace slowed naturally as I gazed at the way the lace-curtained windows of the cabin seemed to be watching my approach, and even the porch's rocking chair seemed to be anticipating my company as it rocked back and forth in the breeze.

Smiling through my tears, I encouraged my mind to take as much time as it needed to imprint the image before me, and promised my heart that I would never forget the woman I had become in the graceful footprint of this place.

MY HAND WAS SHAKING as I handed Roger the card in its white envelope and the little blue vase I had filled with wildflowers gathered on my last walk through the woods. The two of us stood somewhat awkwardly in front of each other. It was still fairly early, and Roger's eyes looked sleepy, as if he had just rolled out of bed. My heart was such a tumble of emotions, I was afraid to speak, not knowing what I might say.

"Thank you, Maria," Roger said quietly, and then handed me the copy of his book. I swallowed hard, trying to hang on to my composure, and nodded. Two fat tears rolled down and dropped off my chin onto the cover. Smiling, Roger dipped his finger into the tiny puddles and then lifted his finger to his lips.

"Aren't you going to read what I wrote?" he asked. I shook my head no, having decided in advance not to read his inscription while we were still together. I wanted to be able to trace the scrawl of his words when he was no longer within reach of my kiss.

Looking into each other's eyes, we were drawn as if by an invisible cord into each other's arms. Closing my eyes, I willed myself to remember everything about this moment, the strength of his arms around my waist, the salty taste of his lips. Finally, impossibly, we released our grip.

"Beauty, Beauty," Roger said softly, caressing my cheek, "you are the sun."

Opening the door to my car, I unzipped my suitcase and placed Roger's book on top of the other special re-membrances I had packed inside: a single red rose he had given me, pressed between the pages of my journal, and the T-shirt I had worn the first time we made love, un-washed and still bearing his scent. Turning back to him, I smiled and blew him a kiss, then climbed into the front seat and pulled the door closed.

Edging the minivan slowly down the dirt drive, I glanced in my rearview mirror and saw Roger, standing with his arms outstretched, head tipped back, reaching in reverence toward the sky. I realized then that his presence in my life was a blessing, a love, goodness, and grace that could only take root and spread. Knowing this, I could say good-bye and move into the rest of my life. His love, like everyone else's I had known—my parents' and siblings', closest friends', Claude's, and especially my kids'—was an integral part of who I was, and no matter where I ended up, all the love I had ever known would always be there.

PART TWO

*Whatever Happened
to Her?*

A NEW LIFE

THE MOON CAST its silvery light over everything, as Claude and I held hands and walked. The low murmur of our conversation strung between us in the thick humidity of the August night, and played against the rhythm of our footfalls and the backdrop of the katydids' thrum. I mostly stared ahead, as the two of us walked, but once in a while, glancing up, I could see moments in the lives of our neighbors, lit and framed in the windows of their houses.

These days, it seemed Claude and I were having only one conversation, which had started almost a month earlier when the kids and I had returned from Michigan, and I had told Claude I wanted a divorce. I wasn't prepared for Claude's response. Rather than being angry or relieved, he had been stunned. The next morning, I had watched quietly from the door of our room as Claude lifted his wedding ring from its spot on his dresser and put it on his finger for the first time in eight months. I could feel it now, pressed against the skin of my fingers, as the two of us held hands.

For the first time in our relationship, even more than when Hannah was sick, Claude and I were being truly honest with each other about who we were and what we wanted for our lives. After so many years of struggling to stay married, it seemed unbelievable that things between us felt so calm. It was as if our fight all this time had been less with each other and more against the inevitability of our divorce. Now, the decision having been made, the relief was both understandable and unavoidable.

As I began to trust what was happening between us, I had not only told Claude about the realizations I had come to about myself and my life in my time away, but also the truth about the extent of my relationship with Roger. Though I knew the disclosure would be extremely painful for both of us, I also believed that Claude deserved to know, to have his suspicions validated, and I also wanted and needed to assume full responsibility for my actions, including the consequences of them.

Once again, I had been surprised by Claude's response. While he had expressed his deep pain in having been betrayed, he had also opened his heart to me and shared the details of a relationship he'd been too ashamed to tell me about many years before. It seemed, in the eighteen years since we'd met, there had been significant shifts in both of us internally, but after all the counseling sessions and date nights, the extent of our growing differences had never been honestly or fully explored. The biggest distinction between us now was that while Claude continued to hold out hope that our relationship might be saved or perhaps reconstellated into some more open form of marriage, I, having made the decision that I needed to divorce, was feeling stronger and clearer in myself every day.

Now, as the two of us walked around and around the block, and Will, Margaret, and Madelaine slept in their beds under a baby-sitter's watchful eye, I felt as close as ever to Claude, but now more as a brother or a friend. Our shared love for our children was still the strongest, purest connection between us, and I felt certain that because of that and because of the way our hearts had finally, understandably, broken open to each other, there was hope we might now be able to create happier lives as individuals and a more respectful and supportive relationship as divorced parents.

GRAVITY

I WAS ROCKING BACK on the legs of my chair, staring at the ceiling, while Claude absently drummed his fingers on the edge of the kitchen table. We had spent the past two hours raising and then shooting down all the custody options we could think of. Now, having reached an impasse, I felt the gravity of our situation begin to settle like lead in the space between us.

For weeks now, we had been trying to decide how to construct our custody arrangement in a way that would address both our children's needs and our individual needs as parents. At first, we had assumed we would do what most divorcing parents do: have the children live with me in our house in Fair Haven during the week and spend weekends and holidays with Claude in a home he would establish close by. But, while the idea of Will, Margaret, and Madelaine remaining in the same house, schools, and community addressed our shared commitment to keeping their everyday lives as stable and predictable as possible, the usual custody model didn't support Claude's and my individual needs as single parents.

Claude wanted everything about his life—his job, his hometown, his church—to remain the same, but I felt less certain. While the prospect of being independent for the first time in my life was both terrifying and exhilarating, because I knew so little about what lay ahead, I felt especially unprepared to support myself, much less our children, financially. I had been out of the corporate world for almost ten years, so the idea of slipping back in felt unrealistic. Besides, what I really wanted was to explore the possibility of finally writing the book about Hannah's life and death. But the real sticking point, besides my uncertainty about the future and Claude's wish to stay in Fair Haven, was that Claude kept insisting he had to see our children every day, or at least be permitted to stop by to tuck them in every night. No matter which way I looked at it, it seemed a bad idea.

Suddenly Claude sat straight up in his chair. I glanced at him, feeling the shift in his energy. Clearing his throat, his eyes as serious as I had ever seen them, he turned to me. "Would you consider reversing the usual way of doing it? I'll stay here, in the house with the kids, as the primary custodian, and you can get a place of your own just down the road."

I felt as if the life was being squeezed out of my heart.

"Are you crazy?" I shouted, jumping up from the table. Part of me couldn't believe he was serious, except the look in his eyes assured me he was. Turning away, I ran up the stairs to our room, taking two steps at a time, feeling as if I couldn't get far enough away from the words that had dropped out of Claude's mouth. Throwing myself on the bed, sobbing into my pillow, I inhaled several deep breaths, trying to restore a sense of order in my frantic mind. The first thing to do, I knew, was to phone my lawyer. I was willing to entertain a lot of new possibilities in my life, but I could never leave my kids.

Unraveled

RELEASE

I LAY IN BED with my eyes open, staring at the dark ceiling. The house was quiet except for Claude's snores and the occasional skitter of a squirrel on the roof above. I sat up, readjusted the bulk of my pillow, and peered at the luminous green hands of the clock on the dresser. It was an hour after midnight. I lay back and closed my eyes one more time, willing myself to sleep.

It had been almost a week since Claude first made his suggestion about retaining primary custody of our children, and although I still felt far from ready to say yes to his suggestion, I had a lot more information about how it might work and what it might mean. My lawyer had been the first to reassure me that there was no need to panic by explaining, in detail, the legal ramifications of such an agreement. It seemed that primary custody in our case didn't have anything to do with which parent was more fit or loving, but rather who the children would be with more days of the year. As long as I re-tained joint legal custody, which Claude and I had agreed I would do, I wouldn't be "giving up" my kids.

Intellectually, as Claude and I began to discuss the de-tails further, I could see how his proposal might make sense. While he and I had, for years, co-created the illu-sion that he was incapable of handling anything to do with the house or the kids for more than a few hours, in truth, I knew he was as capable a parent and householder as I was. With his proposed arrangement and the help of a live-in au pair, he would remain in the more traditional home environment, work, and routine he valued, while I would be able to create a home and career, more sup-portive of the simpler life I now knew I wanted to share with my kids. Claude's plan also eliminated the need for us to sell the house Hannah had died in, something nei-ther of us wanted to do. But more important to both of us was the fact that Will, Margaret, and Madelaine would be able to stay where they were, affording them a sense of continuity that seemed especially important now.

Even so, as my body began to release into sleep, a nameless fear lurked beneath any rational argument I might make. Just before dropping into the dark behind my eyes, I felt a single question float to the surface.

"What am I afraid of?" I asked. Suddenly my eyes flew open, and I sat bolt upright in bed. In an instant, the source of my fear had come clear. The reason I was hesitating to say yes to Claude's proposal wasn't because I was afraid of losing my children's love or because I felt it would mean I was an incompetent mother. The reason I was hesitating to say yes was because I was afraid of what other people would think.

Having seen the source of my resistance to Claude's plan with such clarity, I finally knew what I had to do. No matter how much I wanted to feel loved and respected by my close friends and community, my family's needs were more important. Trusting what I knew as love, I would agree to visitation with my children every other weekend, holidays, and summers, and give primary custody to Claude.

WINGS, LIFTING

WILL AND I were locked and double-locked into a side-by-side harness, as we grinned and gave the Daredevil Dive operator the "thumbs-up." I pulled on the buckles of Will's harness once more, just to be sure, then smiled and waved at Claude and the girls, who were watching us from behind the ticket taker's gate.

The night before, Claude and I had broken the news of our impending divorce to Will, Margaret, and Madelaine, as age-appropriately as we could. All of us had cried. There was no attempt to hide our shared sense of uncertainty and loss. But once the tears had dried, Margaret, having just turned four, and Madelaine, about to turn three, didn't have any questions, while Will had seemed unusually quiet and accepting, as if this was what he had anticipated all along. Now, looking over at him, I felt grateful that Claude had taken the day off so we could take a break from the intensity of what was happening at home, and also give our children a sense that a family was still a family, even if divorced.

"Are you scared, Mom?" Will asked, his eyes bright and wild as the hoist began to lift our bodies off the ground. I grabbed his hand and held on, knowing it wouldn't prevent us from falling if something went terribly wrong, but wanting to reassure him that he was not alone.

"Not yet," I said, grinning, "but I will be when we get to the top!"

As our feet left the asphalt, we pitched forward like birds, arms outstretched as wings, facing the ground. Rows of spectators, who were lined up along fences on either side, began waving and calling out words of encouragement. I kept my eyes on Claude and the girls, who seemed to be making the most noise. Gradually, as the hoist pulled us higher, the details of the faces of those on the ground began to blur, the sounds of their voices grew fainter, and our eyes became more focused on the spectacular view of the amusement park spreading across the landscape below. When I thought we could go no higher, the hoist continued its climb. I felt my heart begin to race like a rabbit in my chest, and looking at Will's face, I saw the first trace of fear in his eyes.

"I think I'm scared now, Mom," he said, quieter now.

"Yes, Will, I am too," I replied, knowing that a more

honest thing had never been said. "This is one of those moments in our lives when we're simply going to have to trust that everything is okay. And while we do that, let's also take a moment to appreciate how amazing it is that we are this high, this excited, and this brave together."

Suddenly there was a loud, grinding noise as our bodies bounced slightly up and down on the ends of the tethers, our momentum having continued upward even though the operator had halted our climb. Below us, the amusement park was splayed out in bright lights and colors, and far off in the distance, I could see a highway, threaded with beads of cars, snaking across green flatland, toward the sea.

"Wow!" Will exclaimed, his fear forgotten now. "This is so great! Thank you, Mom, for doing this with me."

"Thank you, Will," I said, smiling and squeezing his hand.

"Ground control to flyers one and two," the operator called to us over the loudspeaker, "When you're ready, pull the cord."

I turned to Will. "Do it, Mom," he said, his eyes full of excitement again. Reaching above my head, I felt for the handle the guy had shown me before we left the ground.

"Three, two, one," I said aloud, and then pulled as

hard as I could on the cord. Even though I had initiated our release, my body was still caught off guard. I felt my stomach lurch into the back of my throat and the skin on my face stretched back by the air rushing past, my form weightless in free fall. A sound I could describe only as a roar of delight pushed its way out of my chest, as Will and I, still holding hands, felt the straps of the harness stop our fall, then lightly bounce back, sending us flying now, swinging out over the cheering crowd and back. I caught a glimpse of Margaret's face as we rushed past, blurred because of our speed, but enough in focus to catch her wide grin.

"Yippee!!" Will screamed, waving his arms at the crowd now, "I'm flying!"

As the arc of our swing began to shorten and slow, I became aware of my breath again, and felt the river of blood coursing through my body. I had never felt so instantly, so fully alive in my life. And I could see from Will's reaction, he felt the same way. I knew that this moment I had shared with him was the first of many "firsts" we were going to experience together in the months and years ahead, and I could only hope that we would both continue to trust life and each other the way we had moments ago.

SCARLET LETTER

MY FRIEND KIM was standing in front of me, her
hands on her hips, eyes dark and flashing. "What makes
you think you're so special?" she said. "Don't you think
all of us are tired and bored with our lives at times? We're
sticking it out, though. Why can't you?"

The two of us were standing on either side of the island in her newly remodeled kitchen. Her boys and my
girls were playing together in the next room. Although I
had mentally prepared for the responses I might receive
when people first heard the news about the decision
Claude and I had made about custody, standing mute in
front of Kim, I felt as if I had been struck, full force, on
the face. More and more, it was beginning to feel as if I
were once again in a stare-down between what people
wanted for me and what I wanted for myself. I had not
realized until now how much courage it takes to show
your dreams to someone else.

I had expected people's judgment of me to be harsh and unrelenting, especially since I had decided early on not to deny that I had had a sexual relationship with Roger while on my retreat. After all, it hadn't been that long ago when I, too, had believed that adultery was a mortal sin. But I had also hoped that my newfound sense of happiness and peace would at least assuage the doubt of my closest friends. I was wrong. Instead, my friendships, left and right, seemed to be dying slow, painful deaths. I was not only Hester Prynne, unashamedly wearing a scarlet letter, being shut out of a community of people I had come to love and trust—I was Hester Prynne, unashamedly wearing a scarlet letter, who had given up her kids. As far as most people were concerned, nothing could be worse.

Now, facing Kim, I searched my heart for the right, best words to explain why I still believed everything was okay, to reassure her that Claude and I had made our custody decision *because* we loved our kids.

"Remember the book we all read a few summers ago, *The Bridges of Madison County,* the story of the woman who had the brief, three-day love affair with the dashing, worldly photographer while her husband and children were away?" Kim nodded, her expression grim.

"Well, what happened to me was something like that. In spending so much time on my own and then meeting and loving Roger, I discovered parts of myself that I have always known but had almost forgotten, parts of myself that are alive, beautiful, and necessary aspects of the woman I am." Kim, glancing at the long, flowing skirt and scarf I had begun wearing now that I was an incense-burning, meditating, pioneer woman, looked skeptical. Boldly I continued on.

"Unlike the woman in the book, though, I do not want to shove the kitchen table on which I once made passionate love into the basement and hide the love letters for my children to find after I'm dead. I truly believe that those I love, especially and most importantly, my children, deserve to know the best of who I am and who I am capable of being while I am alive and able to share it with them." I took a deep breath, trying to gauge Kim's response. She had relaxed her stance, but still looked disapproving.

"Good for you," she said. "What about your kids, then? Why can't you do all this and have them live with you?"

It was a fair question, and I knew it. But I also knew that this was the aspect of the decision I had made that I still found difficult to explain. No matter how I said it, even to myself, it sounded self-centered and shortsighted. But I knew in my heart that my gift in this world was more as an artist than an everyday kind of mother. And my real responsibility to my life, the lives of my children, and the world, was for me to have the courage to create a sense of home and work that would allow me time to explore and express the things I wondered about and knew.

But, looking into Kim's still angry eyes, I didn't have the courage in that moment to say it to her face. Instead, I simply said, "Even if it isn't obvious to anyone else, I deeply trust that Claude and I are doing what is best for our children and our family. Beyond that, I have nothing to say."

Kim glared at me, then turned on her heel and stomped into the other room. I expected to feel like crying, but instead, I felt a deep calm settling into my bones. I knew in that moment that people, no matter who they were, were better judges of their own fears than they could ever be of me.

APARTMENT BY THE SEA

WILL AND MARGARET scrambled up the steps ahead of me, while Claude, carrying Madelaine, followed close behind. This was the third apartment we had seen that day. Already I liked this one best. Three miles from what we were already calling "Daddy's house," it was situated on a thin peninsula of land, with views of the river and boat harbor on one side, and the expanse of beach and ocean on the other.

"Whoa, Mom, this is a good one," Will said, having reached the top of the stairs.

"Yes, Mommy, let's get it," Margaret chimed in, jumping up and down and clapping her hands.

Stepping into the living area, I stopped and turned slowly, taking it all in. The ad in the paper had said the one-bedroom apartment was full of light, furnished, and spacious. I was pleased to see that they were right on all counts. The living room and dining room were one space, flooded with sun from a large window and sliding glass door that showcased the views and led to a small terrace. The space was carpeted and furnished with a comfortable blue sleeper sofa, two beige, upholstered chairs that folded out into twin-sized beds, a rocking chair, coffee table, and a rattan and glass-topped dining room set.

I followed Claude into the bedroom. A queen-sized platform bed stood in the center of the room, flanked by two rows of bookshelves on either side. A large walk-in closet and dresser stood opposite two large windows that overlooked the sea. Crossing the small hall, I peeked my head into the bathroom. Everything seemed perfect, simple, well cared for, and clean. Although it was small, it was beautiful. Already I could picture myself walking the beach every morning, capturing the colors of the sea in paint, writing at the small café table on the terrace, and inviting friends for dinner in the evenings. This place, I knew, could easily be my own, first home, the perfect place for my kids and me.

"What do you think?" I asked Claude, turning and smiling at him.

"I think this is your decision to make," he replied, more seriously than I. The tone of his voice caught my attention, and I paused, staring for a moment into his now clearly sad eyes. My heart sank as I felt how hard this must be for him. I was so full of my own sense of excitement and anticipation about the changes I was now making in my life, I often forgot how painful it still was for Claude. I had released my hold on the dream we had once shared, but he, it seemed, was holding out hope that things between us were eventually going to ease back toward intimate relationship, with the same hope that had kept him praying for Hannah's recovery until her final breath.

THUD

THE RIGHT TURN SIGNAL LIGHT was blinking on the car's console as I waited for traffic to clear. Margaret was in the front passenger seat next to me, which was an unusual treat for both of us, since I usually insisted for safety reasons that she and Madelaine ride in the backseat. Today, though, I had permitted the exception, as she and I were on our way to have lunch at a restaurant, just the two of us. These days, knowing I would be moving out of the house soon, I was making a specific point to spend time individually with each of the kids.

"Mommy," Margaret asked quietly, "am I the reason you and Daddy are getting divorced?"

Instantly, I forgot all about the traffic on the road in front of me. Pulling the car over onto the shoulder and coming to a stop, I put the emergency flashers on. Reaching across the front seat, I gathered Margaret into my arms and felt tears welling up in my eyes as I buried my face in her hair. I had expected and encouraged my children to ask questions of me, but no book or idea could have prepared me for how much it would hurt to see Margaret, at four years old, so wise and yet in so much pain.

"Margaret," I said with conviction, "You are definitely *not* the reason Dad and I are getting divorced. And I am so sorry that you even had to wonder about that."

I felt Margaret's body relax in my arms as she began to sob. Her arms reached around my neck and pulled me closer. She felt so small and vulnerable, cuddled up against me in my lap. Each of my children had a special place in my heart, unique to him or her. Margaret was the baby who had grown in my body in the last year of Hannah's life. It was she I had talked to as I caressed my swollen belly in the middle of the night, in the dark of Hannah's hospital room. Because of Margaret, I had known there was still a reason to hope and live in those impossible months of waiting for Hannah's death.

Now, running my fingers through her hair and kissing the tears from her cheeks, I prayed for strength and wisdom as a mother, wanting more than anything to know that I was truly making the best, right decisions not only for me but also for our family, for my kids.

MOMMY ALWAYS COMES BACK

TEARS WERE STREAMING down my cheeks as I held Will and then Margaret and Madelaine close enough to my body to imprint their scents on my heart. Gradually, as each of them released their grip, I knew it was time for me to go. Claude hadn't been able to say good-bye. Instead, he had chosen to wait just inside the door of the house. Smiling now through my tears, I encouraged Will, Margaret, and Madelaine to join him. I didn't want their last memory of me in that house to be of watching me drive away.

Giving each of them one last hug, I whispered in their ears, "Remember, I love you, and Mommy always comes back." All three of them smiled at the reminder.

"We love you, Mommy," Madelaine said. Will, his eyes too close to tears, nodded, as Margaret threw her arms around my legs. "I love you, Mommy," she said.

Even though my heart was threatening to break open and bleed all over the driveway, I smiled and waved to the three of them as they went into the house and closed the door. Climbing into the car, I willed my tears to remain inside until I got to my apartment, knowing I would have plenty of time to cry on my own then. As I backed out of the drive, I glanced quickly into the backseat at the two suitcases of clothes and six boxes of items I had decided to bring with me, including an album of photographs, a blanket of Hannah's and a few drawings she had made, several CDs of favorite music, and my books and journals.

Driving away from everything I loved and knew best, the weight of my body felt impossibly heavy, and yet I also felt lighter and free in a way I would have been ashamed to admit out loud. I had taken almost nothing from our home, wanting my life to be as simple and uncomplicated as possible. And though Claude had offered to cover my expenses for the next month, including my groceries and the cost of a rental car, until the divorce was final and the small settlement we had agreed on came through, I hadn't taken a dime more than I thought I might need in order to get back on my feet.

Now, driving alongside the breakwater, I rolled down the window and inhaled the mist blowing in off the shore. Without knowing how anything was going to turn out, good or bad, in the future, I felt relieved, even elated, that I was finally and irreversibly committed to the life I had once only dreamed about, a life that now seemed to be dreaming me.

WISH UPON A STAR

I WOKE TO THE WARMTH of the morning sun pouring through the open window onto my face. Shading my eyes, I sat up in bed, careful not to wake the girls, who were sleeping on either side of me. I slowly lifted my body from under the covers and swung my feet over onto the floor, mindful of Will, who was asleep on the fold-out mattress.

I padded into the kitchen, switched the coffeemaker on, and made myself a piece of toast. I heard footfalls behind me and turned in time to see Will, in baggy flannel pajama bottoms, his hair tousled from a good night's sleep, shuffling into the bathroom. Minutes later, as I sipped my coffee and nibbled toast, staring out the window at the spread of the sun across the open water, Margaret, followed by Madelaine, came flying into the room, all morning sweetness and giggles, and fell across my lap. Covering them with kisses, I pointed toward the sea.

"How about a morning walk along the beach?" I asked, smiling gratefully at Will, who was already setting the table for breakfast, pouring milk into bowls of cereal, and filling glasses with juice.

"Yes, yes, yes," all three shouted.

Half an hour later, our pockets stuffed with gallon-sized freezer bags we used to hold beach treasures, the four of us were trudging across the dunes toward the edge of the water. Our progress was slow because the girls were already bent over, sifting through the sand, scooping up handfuls of shells. As we crested the highest dune and began our descent toward the waves, I caught my breath.

"Look, Mom," Will exclaimed.

There, spread out across the sand like a mirror image of the night sky, were hundreds and hundreds of starfish, which had washed up on shore. Margaret and Madelaine ran up to stand beside me and gasped when they saw the beautiful sight. Slowly, the four of us moved closer. I could see now that some of the creatures were still alive, the pointed tips of their bony arms moving over the sand. Two crusty old fishermen seated in beach chairs behind their fishing poles saw us approaching.

"Never saw anything like it," one of them said.

I wanted to kneel in front of the miraculous happening and cry for the bittersweetness of so much beauty and death in one breath. I watched as the girls and Will began to step carefully through the starry expanse. Finally, unable to contain her curiosity, Margaret carefully lifted one of the lifeless forms, running one finger over its rippled edges and studying its underside.

"Oh, Mommy," she cried, "it's so sad. I think it's dead." Lowering the starfish into the water, she crouched on her heels, carefully watching for signs of movement. After a minute or so, she lifted it back. Madelaine, standing quietly behind her, turned to me.

"Mommy, can we take the dead ones home and put them in the bathtub? We have to try to save them," she said.

I looked at Will, who was already running down the beach, tossing the starfish that were still alive back into the sea. Nodding my head yes, I was reminded in that moment of the way my children had always been my best teachers, and I felt blessed to be able to witness a sense of hope and possibility as innocent and beautiful as theirs.

RETURNING

I STEPPED OUT of the shower and stared at my image in the mirror. I knew that the woman looking back at me was the same woman who had brought four children into the world, had held Hannah's dying body in her arms, and had loved more than one man. She was also now a woman living on her own, sharing her life with her children on weekends, holding a world of possibilities in her hands.

Reaching for the bottle of Eternity that now sat on the edge of my bathroom sink, I smiled, thinking of Roger, as I dabbed it on. Days before, I had made a special trip to the mall to purchase this reminder of him. Now, inhaling its scent, I wondered if the changes I had made since we'd last been together, my new independence and confidence, would be obvious to him. Loosening the towel wrapped around my body, I allowed it to drop to the floor. As I stared at my nakedness in the mirror and saw all the ways I was not getting younger, I decided it was time to e-mail him.

TREMORS

I WAS SITTING in a patch of autumn sun, halfway up a rise in the park lawn, just across the path from the Boathouse in Central Park, where Roger and I had agreed to meet. My body was already trembling with anticipation, wondering what it was going to be like to see him, to be with him, for the first time in the everyday world.

My eyes scanned the crowds of people pouring by, mothers and fathers pushing babies in strollers, kids on Rollerblades, streamlined bicyclists, and the occasional jogger. Suddenly I saw him, strolling at a leisurely pace toward the Boathouse gate, wearing white linen trousers and a bright blue, long-sleeved shirt. My legs felt too weak to stand on. I watched as he stopped at the entrance to the restaurant, and glanced around. Seeing him check his watch, I remembered its large round face, black Roman numerals, and well-worn tan leather band.

I knew I couldn't make him wait forever, but I was struggling to catch my breath. My eyes were glued to him now, oblivious to the activity that had kept me occupied only moments before. Finally, I took a deep breath and stood. Steadying myself, I began to walk toward him. I was three paces away when he saw me.

"Hello, Beauty," he said, opening his arms. I could not even speak. My eyes full of tears, I felt his arms encircle my trembling body, coming to rest in the small of my back, pulling me close. My head on his shoulder, he held me there, quietly, firmly, until finally I turned my face to his and gently kissed his lips, which tasted just as I remembered.

Taking my hand, Roger began to lead me along the path, the way he had come. I felt steadier on my feet now, and my head had cleared. Suddenly, Roger stopped and turned toward me. He gazed into my eyes, opening and closing his mouth as if he were trying to say something but couldn't find the words. Finally he spoke.

"Who *are* you?" he asked. As I gazed back at him, smiling, my answer rose from the center of my heart, as clear as his eyes and true.

"I am the second half of your life," I said.

CALIFORNIA

THE PACIFIC OCEAN was spread out before me, an endless expanse of lapis blue. From our vantage point on the top of Mt. Tamalpais, Roger and I could see San Francisco, a city of white nestled into the bay, and the Golden Gate Bridge, its red supports jutting skyward, strung like a necklace with cables. Behind us and below, majestic redwoods created cathedrals of light and shade, filling the canyon with their pungent, earthy scent.

My life had finally brought me to California. I was scheduled to stay for twelve days, visiting Roger. He had recently moved into a little tree house sixty-five steep steps up a mountain, overlooking a redwood canyon. Although San Francisco was often cloaked in drizzly fog, Larkspur, across the bay, where Roger's house was located, seemed always to be bathed in sun. Having endured fifty-three years of English gray, Roger was in bliss. It helped, too, that just down the road there was a lovely

Italian café called Rulli's, a French restaurant, the Left Bank, and an independent bookstore.

"I have to bring my kids here," I said, turning to Roger. He smiled and squeezed my hand. "Next summer," I vowed.

Turning to look eastward, toward the soft, golden hills to the east, I tried to wrap my mind around how vast the space was between where I was standing now and the life I had always known. Like those throughout history who endured months and years of hardship in order to pursue elusive, ambitious dreams, I knew I had given up much in the hope that my life and my children's lives might know and experience more. And I knew, too, that my journey was hardly over; in many important ways it had only just begun.

STAR OF BETHLEHEM

THE LITTLE CHRISTMAS TREE, its ball of roots wrapped in burlap and tied with a big red bow, stood in one corner of the living room. Will, Margaret, Madelaine, and I had decorated it earlier with tiny white lights and assorted seashells and starfish, which the girls had hung from the branches using loops of white string. A tinfoil Star of Bethlehem was fastened to the uppermost branch, and a modest assortment of packages, wrapped with butcher-block paper, sponge-painted by Madelaine, were arranged underneath. Across the room, the glass-topped dining room table was covered with cookie crumbs, chocolate sprinkles, and drips of bright-colored frosting, and in the kitchen, Margaret and Madelaine were rolling and cutting more sugar cookies, while Will kept an eye on those already baking.

I stood in the center of the room and smiled. In a little more than three months, it seemed that the kids and I had finally settled into the rhythm of this new life. Though it hadn't been easy for any of us to get used to being separated from each other for days, when we were together now, there was a palpable sense of ease and simplicity between us that was all the more sweet because of the extended absences in between.

"As soon as you three are finished in there, I'll make some hot chocolate to go with those cookies while you put on your pajamas," I said.

"Okay, Mom," the three of them replied in unison.

An hour later, the room dark except for the flickering flame of a candle and the lights on the tree, the four of us were snuggled together on the couch, wrapped in a large down comforter. The room was silent, but in the distance, I could hear the rhythmic pounding of the waves on the shore. Glancing at the tumble of bodies laying across my lap, I saw that while Will was still fighting to keep his eyes open, Margaret's and Madelaine's were already closed.

"Mom," Will whispered, "this might sound funny, but besides the Christmas when Santa gave me Nintendo Sixty-four, I think this might be one of the best Christmases ever." Reaching for his hand under the comforter, I gave it a squeeze.

"I don't think it sounds funny, Will," I whispered back. "In fact, I definitely agree."

MOROCCO

IT WAS CLOSE TO MIDNIGHT as I made my way through the airport in Casablanca, Morocco, trying to find the gate for my flight to Marrakech. It wasn't proving to be as easy as I'd hoped it would be. None of the signs that I could see were written in English. I thought I might stop and ask for directions, but the only other people in sight were men in green uniforms, carrying automatic weapons, patrolling the halls. All of the restaurants and shops along the corridors were closed. Turning a corner, I fell into step alongside a handful of travelers, most wearing robes or business suits, some with headdresses, all carrying luggage. Since they seemed to know where they were going, I decided to follow them.

I was scheduled to meet Roger in Marrakech. He had invited me there, along with a small group of friends, to go on a walking journey he was leading in the Sahara desert. I had immediately said yes. The next day, I bought a beautiful leather duffel bag to use as luggage. I felt certain it would make me look more like the seasoned world traveler I had always imagined myself to be.

Now, though, walking through Casablanca's airport, clutching the bag in my hand, I knew that a cool leather bag does not a seasoned traveler make. I felt particularly conspicuous, a six-foot, two-inch blonde wearing a long, flowered skirt, brown leather boots, and a brown felt cowboy hat I'd ordered from the Boy Scouts catalog when I was Will's cub scout den mother. I hoped I didn't look as lost as I felt. Following the others, I saw that we were approaching the first gate I'd seen that looked open. Airline attendants were scurrying around, checking people in. I handed my ticket to the agent at the counter, assuming that if I were in the wrong place, she would know from my ticket and redirect me. Instead, she barely glanced at it before authoritatively waving me onto the plane.

The flight attendant at the door of the plane smiled and pointed me down the center aisle. It seemed that there was no assigned seating, which wasn't a problem, as there was hardly anyone else on the plane. Spotting a white woman seated on her own, I made my way toward her and sat down. Shoving my bag under the seat, I turned to her.

"Do you speak English?" I asked.

"*Non. Mais je parle français,*" she replied. It had been almost twenty years since I had taken French in high school, but I remembered enough to comprehend what she'd said. Smiling at her, I settled back into my seat, and decided the flight attendant's announcement would soon clear things up. The only thing I really wanted to know was if I was on the plane to Marrakech.

I watched as eight more people filed onto the plane and sat. Finally, the door closed and the flight attendant who had smiled at me when I boarded stood in front and began making announcements on the loudspeaker. From what I could gather, she repeated her greeting and safety instructions in three different languages. The problem for me was that none were in English. As the plane began to taxi away from the gate, I lay my head against the back of my seat and grinned. I could hardly believe this was my life, that I had had the courage to travel so far from everything that was familiar to me. And because of my courage, I felt protected rather than frightened, and was willing to simply trust that I was on the right plane.

Too excited to sleep, I stared out at the dark sky. I saw no sign of civilization, not a single light below. Finally, after about an hour, I spotted a cluster of lights on the ground. The plane circled and landed. I stood, put my hat on my head, and gathered my bags. Following the others, I stepped out of the plane and walked along a narrow corridor, which eventually opened into a large, fluorescent-lit waiting area. As soon as I saw Roger jumping up and down, waving his arms and beaming at me from the other side of the room, I realized that while my life was expanding and opening me to new experiences and places, what I was actually doing was finding my way home.

SCENT OF A WOMAN

I WAS ALONE IN THE HOUSE, wandering from one room to the next, savoring the integrity and beauty of the life that was being lived by my friend Siobhan, as a woman on her own. Every item in her home had clearly been chosen by Siobhan, or given to her by someone who knew her well and had bought the gift with her in mind. There was nothing formulaic or rigid about the way the rooms flowed into each other or the way the items in them fit together. What connected every piece of art, ceramic bowl, or carved wooden chair was that each piece was imbued with a story from Siobhan's life or travels, and therefore was in relationship, through her, with the whole.

Siobhan and I had met through Roger on the Sahara desert trip. Roger and I were now staying with her, in her home in southern California. Although Siobhan and I were the same age, we had lived very different lives.

Siobhan owned a very successful public relations agency in Los Angeles, had traveled the world extensively, and never had children or married. To me, she was the epitome of what was possible when a woman is unapologetically ambitious about her work and dreams, which is what I was wanting more and more to be.

I hoped I wasn't too late.

The day before, I had gone with Roger to the Los Angeles Coliseum for BookExpo America, or BEA, a national booksellers' convention. I had intended to get a sense of whether the book I wanted to write about Hannah's life and death was the kind of book that booksellers and publishers might support. Instead, I had left feeling discouraged and overwhelmed. Wandering up and down aisles of publishers' booths, each one featuring too many new books to count, I had almost lost my nerve to write. How could I possibly expect to compete in an industry already filled to capacity with good ideas and excellent writers?

And yet, as I studied the images of Siobhan in the photographs on her mantel, seeing her life unfold through the lens of a camera across different times and places, I saw a woman who had made a life for herself by trusting what she loved most and best. For me, having given myself time in the past year, since leaving Claude, to explore and discover the kind of life I wanted to live, I knew that writing was what I most wanted to do. Standing in the middle of the beautiful life and space Siobhan had created, I now knew something else was also true. I was not only going to have to write, I was going to have to do everything I could to make a decent living doing it. I did not want to make a life with Roger or anyone else until I knew I was capable of creating and supporting myself and my children on my own.

Unraveled

RIVER OF HEALING

I WAS SITTING on the front porch of my parents'
house in Traverse City, in the same spot where I used to
sit and dream when I was young. Tipping my head back
and closing my eyes, I inhaled the sweet, clean scent of
the breeze blowing across the surface of Lake Michigan.

My father was sick. Months before, he had been diagnosed with cancer. It was a devastating blow. My father
was like a tree that had always lived in the front yard of
my life, strong, invincible, protecting. Morality was his
measure. He was the reason I had always wanted to do
the right thing, to make him proud of me. It was my father who had taught me that I was worthy and beautiful,
not because of my sexuality or because I was a woman,
but because I was who I was. I could not begin to imagine what my life would be like if he died.

These days I was feeling less confident, not only because of my father's illness. My divorce from Claude had

been finalized more than seven months before, and Claude had decided that once the judge's gavel came down, he would no longer speak directly to me. Our only communication, at his request, was by e-mail or through the post office. He had rented a post office box for our correspondence, telling me he didn't want anything of mine coming to his house. At first, I had imagined it was only a temporary setback. But I now knew that the only temporary aspect of our relationship had been the ease with which we had negotiated the months before our divorce.

I was also now seriously considering moving to California. Roger had invited me to live with him, in his tree house in the canyon. Although I felt far from ready to marry again, there was such a joy in our being together, and a nourishing sense of spaciousness and support between us, that living together felt like the next, right step. I also could not imagine living, even for short periods of time, so far from my kids—any more than I could have previously imagined giving primary custody to Claude. But because Roger had dreamed all his life of living in California, just as I had, I couldn't bring myself to ask him to leave and come to New Jersey.

I felt as if my life were once again sucking me into a direction I would never have chosen for myself, away from the way I had always believed it was supposed to be.

And while I trusted the movement because my instincts told me it was right, I also hated that it was throwing me into the limelight again. Moving to California could only confirm what most people already believed, that I had not only divorced Claude, I had abandoned my kids.

And yet, whatever they believed, I also knew it could not change the truth. Since Claude was now making it impossible for me to see my children except during scheduled visitation weekends, it would change almost nothing if I were to live in California during the week and fly back and forth to New Jersey on visitation weekends. Life on two coasts would also mean that Will, Margaret, and Madelaine would be able to live in California with Roger and me every summer, which was an idea that appealed to me too.

Sitting now on the stoop of my parents' house, I could hardly believe how different my life and my children's lives already were from the childhood memories I had made here. I felt lucky to be able to return to the home I had grown up in, to reimmerse myself in the family dynamics that had shaped my earliest ideas of who I was supposed to be, to see my mother and father as well as their relationship through different, more experienced eyes. I understood now that most of my life, my goal had been to do what my parents had done, only better. Now, though, I was beginning to realize that not only was I not them, I was someone with completely different dreams, wanting to explore a world my parents had never known.

I heard the screen door behind me open. Turning, I saw my father, holding two glasses of lemonade, coming toward me.

"Do you mind if I join you, honey?" he asked.

"Not at all, I'd love it," I said.

Perching on the edge of the stoop, he handed me one of the glasses. I took a sip, savoring the tangy sweetness in my mouth before swallowing. My father cleared his throat. I looked at him, realizing now that he had an ulterior motive in joining me. I remained silent, wondering what he was going to say.

"Maria, I need to tell you something," he said finally. My heart leaped into my throat. Suddenly, I was ten years old, anticipating a scolding. My father addressed me by my first name only when it was really serious or important.

"I want to talk with you about your life and the decisions you've made and are making." He cleared his throat again and took another sip of lemonade. My heart was now thudding in my chest. I willed myself to stay focused on my father's words. "What I have to say," he continued, "isn't just about you or your children. It's also about my mother."

His mother! Although he had always found it painful

to speak of her, I knew that my father had always loved his mother deeply. For years he had kept a large, framed photograph of her on top of a table in his office. I could see her image now, in my mind, a dark-haired woman with pale skin, full lips, and deep feeling eyes, wearing a formal-looking, light-colored suit with a wide-brimmed hat. I knew from what I had overheard as a child that she was a quiet, soft-spoken woman who had been loved by everyone who knew her, and the wife of a doctor, my father's father, an intense, emotionally abusive, alcoholic man. The source of my father's profound sorrow was that she had died in the hospital of cancer when my father was sixteen, before my father and his brothers were even told she was sick.

My father was speaking. "Honey, I want you to know that, in terms of the decisions you've made in your life this past year, even the difficult one you're considering now, I think you're doing the right thing. It hasn't been easy, I know, to have the kind of courage you've had. But for those of us who love you, and especially Will, Margaret, and Madelaine, it is wonderful to see you putting yourself out there. God gives each of us talents to express. Whose right is it to limit the expression of those gifts? I feel lucky to have you as a daughter, and I will always be committed to instilling in you your right to excel."

I wanted to cry, my heart swelling with gratitude and relief, but my father was not done.

"This has always been a man's world," he continued. "And no one knew that more than my mother. But she didn't have the strength to do what you're doing. She put up with a lot of unhappiness and abuse, and it killed her." He hesitated. I waited. "What I have to say next might sound strange to most people, but I am sure you will understand. I still feel my mother. Her presence has always been a part of my life. And what I feel in relation to her now is that the decisions you're making as a woman are not only helping you and your children. Your decisions are also healing her."

I was stunned. I had never heard my father speak like this. As his words sank into my bones, I felt my need to be perfect in his eyes melting. I knew then that I had to be willing to endure the disapproval of others in order to be everything I was capable of being. My father had reminded me that not only was I responsible to my own life and the lives of my children, but I was responsible to every woman who had come before me and to those who would come after, who needed to be reminded, as I once had, that they are deserving and capable of more.

WHERE THERE'S SMOKE . . .

THE GIRLS WERE ALREADY ASLEEP in the tent. The night sky, stretched over the flat prairie, was dotted with stars. Will and I were savoring the quiet as we took turns poking the smoldering logs of the campfire with sticks. Having already visited the battlefield at Gettysburg, stayed a night in a roadside motel in Illinois, and then continued on to the St. Louis arch, we were now camped by the side of a shallow lake, beneath a willow tree, in the middle of Kansas. Earlier today, after almost a week of traveling, Will had turned to me and asked, "What day is this anyway?" I knew then that we had finally arrived at the wonderful, magical moment when a vacation truly begins.

The four of us were traveling west to California, our luggage, camping equipment, and coolers of food packed tightly into the trunk of the little two-door BMW I had recently purchased, the first car I had ever owned. We had begun our trip with a prayer on the beach in New Jersey. Wading into the Atlantic Ocean, in the same spot where we had gathered starfish months before, each of us had chosen a rock or shell to bring with us, intending to drop them as a greeting into the Pacific as soon as we reached California. Before leaving, we had also stopped at the tree that had been planted in front of our church in Hannah's memory, untied a pink-red heart from its branches, and hung it on our rearview mirror.

Staring into the licking dance of the fire, I listened to the sounds of the prairie around us: the wind in the willow, the chirping of crickets, and the rustling of grass as small (I hoped) animals passed by. Suddenly, Will banged his stick hard on the ground.

"Mom, why did you lie to me?" he asked.

Shocked by the angry tone of his voice and the sudden shift in the air between us, I was temporarily tongue-tied.

"What do you mean, Will?" I managed to say.

"You promised me you and Dad wouldn't get a divorce," he replied, glaring at me, his eyes filling with tears.

I felt my heart soften as I studied his face, trying to decide what to say. I could still remember when he was a baby, growing inside me, the way, when his heel was digging into my ribs, I simply had to touch him where it hurt and his whole body would gently shift. Now, at eleven and a half, he was a young man, almost taller than me, with my eyes, his dad's lips, and an already broken-open heart. Hannah's death as well as the divorce had shattered his innocence. He knew things about life that no one his age, or perhaps any age, should know.

"I am so sorry, Will," I began, choosing my words carefully. "I can't even begin to imagine how painful Dad's and my divorce must feel to you." I paused, wanting to get the next part exactly right.

"But I don't remember my promise the same way you do." I saw the shift in his gaze. He was eyeing me suspiciously now. I took a deep breath.

"What I remember promising you is that Dad and I were going to do everything we could to avoid getting divorced. But in the end, we weren't able to work things out."

Will was silent for a moment, as if he were calculating the differences between his memory and mine in his head. Finally he nodded.

"Yeah, I guess that is what you said," he agreed, kicking dirt into the fire with his foot. "I probably just remembered it the way I *wished* you had said it." It was my turn to nod in agreement. I waited, allowing him a moment with his thoughts, and then reached out to touch his arm.

"I'm still sorry, though, Will," I said quietly. "Divorce is not easy for anyone. Dad and I knew that, which is why we tried so hard for so long to try to make our marriage work. But I also know now that, whatever Dad and I thought divorce would be like, we had no way of knowing how much it would hurt you and the girls."

At that, Will's face crumpled, and I took him into my arms. Rocking him back and forth on my lap, I held him until his sobs subsided and his body softened.

"I'm sorry I was mad at you, Mom," he whispered. I smiled and gave him a hug.

"You don't need to apologize for your feelings, Will," I said. "I'd much rather have you be honest with me than nice. I'm your mother, and that means that I love you no matter what—no matter what you feel, no matter what you do. What is also important to remember, though, as you begin to make decisions in your life is that, over time and with experience, your dreams may change, just as what you believe and what you need will change too."

Holding Will and feeling the words I had just spoken resonating in me, I realized that Will wasn't the only one who needed to be reminded of my message. Having given myself permission to change what I had always believed about myself and my life, I now understood that no matter what I did as a result, staying married or getting divorced, living in New Jersey or moving to California, I was simply exchanging one set of joys and challenges for another, different set. One life wasn't necessarily better or worse than another; it was simply different.

PENTHOUSE IN LAS VEGAS

THE GIRLS WERE JUMPING up and down in the middle of the king-sized bed while Will, already wearing one of the hotel's thick terry-cloth robes, pressed the buttons on the remote control and watched the giant television screen rise out of the credenza in front of him.

"Mom, this is the coolest place *ever!*" he exclaimed.

I had to agree, although at this point, almost anyplace with a bathtub would have excited me. After three days of camping in the Grand Canyon, and more than two and a half weeks on the road, I was ready for some pampering. And this was definitely the right place for that: the penthouse suite at the Mirage Hotel and Casino in Las Vegas. One of Will's requests, when our trip began, was that we stay one night in an extra-fancy hotel. I had explained all of this, including the story of our cross-country trek, to the guy at the front desk. Smiling, he had handed me a special key to the elevator.

"It's a slow day for us," he said, "so I'll only charge you a hundred twenty dollars, the regular room rate. Enjoy."

Even I hadn't known what to expect when the elevator doors opened. I'm certain my mouth must have dropped open, and the kids' did. Stepping into a cavernous marble foyer lined with gilt-edged mirrors and hung with a gigantic crystal chandelier, we had set our luggage on the floor as the elevator doors silently slid shut behind us. The suite contained a formal living room, a dining room with seating for ten, two bedrooms, and a bathroom almost big enough to hold the whole of Roger's house.

Immediately, the girls had begged to be allowed to swim in the bathtub. It was that big. While the water ran into the marble swimming pool, Margaret uncapped two bottles of bubble bath and poured them in. Within minutes, to the girls' delight, the tub looked like a wedding cake with frothy white frosting. Meanwhile, Will was running through the place, looking in every closet, pressing every button he could find. Standing at the expanse of floor-to-ceiling windows that lined the whole of one wall, listening to the giggles of the girls in the bath and the blaring of the surround sound television Will was watching, I gazed out at the courtyard of palm trees, tiki bars, and swimming pools below and the massive range of mountains in the distance.

I could hardly believe that our journey across the

country was almost over. In two days we were scheduled to arrive in Malibu, to stay a few days with Siobhan and drop our shells and stones from the Atlantic into the Pacific. Then, after a few days in Los Angeles, we would head up the winding coast on Highway One to San Francisco and Roger.

Turning from the window, I strolled across to the bathroom, where the commotion had gotten even louder. As I stepped through the door, I laughed out loud when I saw what the girls were doing. Standing in front of the long stretch of mirrors, the two of them, speaking to each other in exaggerated English accents, were dabbing themselves with white powder puffs they had found in a container on the sink, and rubbing handfuls of lotion all over their bodies.

"Don't we smell pretty, Mommy?" Madelaine asked, turning to smile at me.

"Let's call Dad. I want to tell him about how fancy we are," Margaret said.

"Okay, no problem," I said. "I've seen about seven phones in this place. I'm sure there must be at least one in here."

Suddenly Madelaine's smile faded and morphed into a pout. "I miss my daddy," she said.

"Oh, baby, of course you do," I replied, sweeping her into my arms.

"Divorce is no fun," Madelaine continued, her voice

muffled now as her face was buried in my neck. "I'm always missing somebody. When I'm with Daddy, I miss you. And when I'm with you, I miss Daddy."

Will, overhearing Madelaine's words, came and stood in the doorway. Margaret, patting Madelaine's back, said soothingly, "I know it's hard, Maddy. Sometimes, when parents are divorced, you cry because your mom or dad goes on a trip, or has to go swimming or to the restaurant by themselves. But it's not all sad. Because our mommy and daddy are divorced, we now get to have two houses and two bedtimes and lots of adventures. And at night, we don't have to decide which parent gets to read us a story, get us drinks, and turn on the hall light."

Madelaine nodded, raising her head from my shoulder and wiping her eyes. Will came over to her and bent down, stroking her cheek.

"I understand that you feel sad, Maddy," he said, quietly, "but as hard as it is for us now that Mom and Dad are divorced, it was much harder for our whole family when they were living together. I know you don't remember, but I do."

Surprised by his words, and grateful, I turned to him. Will stood up, smiling, and winked at me.

WINDOW BOX IN THE CANYON

I LIT THE VOTIVE CANDLE on my desk, and sat down in the antique oak chair. I was now officially living in California with Roger, and had begun writing a proposal for my book. I already knew the title was *Hannah's Gift,* and that Hannah's favorite red patent leather Mary Janes would be on the cover. What I didn't know, though, was whether I would ever be able to find a publisher willing to publish it, much less pay me any money for it. But while my finances were a reality that desperately needed to be addressed, I wasn't thinking about that now.

My desk was nestled into a windowed nook in our bedroom, with views of the redwoods in the canyon below. With its soft pine top and curved iron legs, it looked writerly and elegant, just as I had hoped it would. I had a new laptop computer, too, and a small silver lamp with a fluted glass shade. In one corner of the desk were a stack of books by some of my favorite poets and writers—Annie Dillard, Mary Oliver, Annie Lamott, and Jane Hirshfield—and photographs of Will, Hannah, Margaret, and Madelaine in carved silver frames.

These days, everything in my life felt as if it was in support of everything else. And although there were many nights when I cried myself to sleep, missing my kids, I also felt that, everything considered, the transition had been mostly transparent for all of us. Will, Margaret, Madelaine, and I still saw each other according to the visitation schedule Claude and I had originally agreed to. And traveling back and forth to New Jersey every other weekend, although expensive, was easier than I had expected. The four of us spent our time together in a lovely furnished but unused apartment of a friend on the Upper East Side of Manhattan. If the New York apartment wasn't available, we sometimes stayed at a hotel with a pool or with our good friends the Lores, whose children were the same ages as mine.

Life with Roger was proving to be a graceful one. Our differences, which at one time had intimidated me, now served as fuel for the conversations we loved to have, and as a basis for the life we were making together. In the months since I had moved in, his friends had quickly become ours. Drinking coffee each morning in the café, returning home to write, read, walk in the canyon, or simply think quietly on the deck overlooking the trees, I had quickly acclimated to a quieter, more thoughtful pace. Evenings were more lively as the two of us went out to dinner at a restaurant, or hosted a gathering at home with friends.

Sitting at my desk, staring at the blinking cursor on my computer screen, I paused. This was always my favorite time of the day, the morning, when every word that was going to emerge onto the page in the next few hours hung expectantly in the air. Writing about Hannah was a joy, but it was also a return to the deepest pain I had ever known. The grief I still felt, though familiar now, was a yawning hole in me. Like the Grand Canyon, it could be crossed only in good weather, at select, narrow places, with no distractions. As my fingers began to pick their way across the keyboard, I felt a sense of elation, as if I were finally, quite literally, taking my life in my hands.

DEATH VALLEY

THE SUN'S HEAT was creating shimmering waves on the surface of Death Valley's arid salt flats. My den mother cowboy hat, the same one I'd worn in the Sahara, afforded my only protection, shading my eyes as I walked. Row upon row of mountains receded into the distance in lighter and lighter shades of gray on either side, but the horizon stretched endlessly in front of us.

Rowan, a filmmaker and new friend of mine in California, had teamed up with Simone, a television personality for MTV-Europe, to make a documentary of ten women journeying through the desert. Originally she had asked Roger to organize it, but as he was already scheduled to be in the Sahara at the same time, he had suggested that I lead the trip. Because he and I had already done a similar journey together, with another group of people in Death Valley earlier in the year, I felt up to the task, and excited, too. If nothing else, I needed the money. The reserves I had saved from my settlement with Claude were quickly dwindling.

The women and I had set up our base camp three days before. Each morning, after breakfast, we cleaned up camp, packed lunches, and filled our canteens with water, then headed out. Everything was done in silence, including the filming, which was being done by an all-woman crew. In the evening, though, after the dinner dishes had been washed and put away, I built a fire in the stone pit. As the sun set behind the mountains and the dark descended on our camp, opening up the starry night sky, each woman was invited to speak about what she had experienced that day.

It was a particularly poetic and powerful experience for me because I was seeing with my own eyes the strength and beauty of what women can accomplish together, when united by a shared intention. I had been particularly moved by the way each of us, without discussing it, had willingly packed and carried extra food, water, and medical supplies each morning, just in case. There was a way, too, that the wildness of the land and the intensity of the elements had shorn us of any pretense and fostered a deep sense of trust between us.

Today, walking with the others, my well-worn leather boots leaving prints in the white, salty sand, not unlike those left by astronauts on the moon, part of me was secretly hoping to find an undiscovered relic from one of the wagon trains I knew had crossed here. The return to my pioneer fantasy and my sense of relationship with the timeless story of human beings striking out in new directions, willing to endure hardship in the process, was deeper than ever in me. My move to California had been the last straw for most of my friendships in New Jersey. Anyone who had been holding out hope that I might eventually come to my senses was now convinced that I truly was crazy.

Now, crossing one of the most extreme expanses on earth, carrying only a small pack and a bottle of water, I knew that, if anything, my life was wanting more and more experiences like this one, where I would be stretched beyond my self-imposed limitations. The best moments of my life had been lived outside and beyond other people's ideas of what I should do, and I was no longer concerned about being considered crazy. Safe, I now knew, was someone else's idea of a life, not mine.

A CRY IN THE DARK

MY EYES WERE CLOSED, but I was not asleep. I lay
quietly, listening to the faraway cries of birds in the
canyon, to the nearer sounds of trashcans being dragged
to the curb and car doors slamming as neighbors left for
work. I turned onto my side and tried to remember what
I had just been dreaming, while Roger, burrowed under
the covers next to me, began to snore.

Suddenly, I heard a loud shout.

"Mom!" A single word, in Will's voice.

I opened my eyes and sat bolt upright in bed, momentarily blinded by the light of the risen sun pouring through
the uncurtained windows. I glanced at the clock on my
desk: 7:45 A.M. My mind was confused, knowing, as I did,
that Will and the girls weren't with us in California; they
were in New Jersey with Claude. Roger, aware of the sudden movement, blinked his eyes open and glanced at me.

"What's wrong?" he asked, sleepily.

"I just heard Will's voice calling me," I replied. "I think something's happened."

Roger stared at me, his brow creased doubtfully.

"Are you sure?" he said, finally. "Maybe you were dreaming."

"No, I wasn't dreaming," I said quietly, my heart thumping wildly in my chest. "It was Will."

I slipped out of bed and padded across the carpet to the phone on my desk. Quickly I dialed Claude's number. I inhaled a few deep breaths as I held the receiver to my ear, hoping someone would pick up. When I heard the answering machine click on, I hung up. Five minutes later I tried again. Nothing.

I felt myself beginning to panic and then, just as suddenly, felt silly. Surely, if something bad had happened, someone would call, if not Claude, then his au pair, Julia. Reminding myself that when I had first moved out of Claude's house, I had made sure the Fair Haven police knew how to reach me, I felt my heart grow quieter and gradually resume its normal rhythm.

I made my way to the bathroom, showered, and then ate breakfast. Every half hour or so, I called Claude's house. Part way through the morning, I glanced at the calendar above my desk and realized it was one of the odd days in the year when the kids were off from school. That would explain it, I thought to myself. Most likely,

Julia had taken everyone to the beach for the day. By lunchtime, still getting no answer, I left a message.

The day passed slowly as I kept watching the clock, waiting for the phone to ring. Finally, just as Roger and I were sitting down to dinner, a call came through. Leaping up, I raced downstairs to my desk, taking the steps two at a time. Picking up the receiver, I said "Hello," more as a question than a greeting.

"Mom, it's me, Will."

"Thank God," I said, before I could stop myself. "I've been worried about you all day."

"Yeah, you must have heard. I had a really bad accident on my bike this morning. Me and my friends were riding and I hit a bump funny and fell off. I don't really remember it, though, because as soon as my head hit the ground, I went unconscious. Someone called 911 and the ambulance came and took me to the hospital. I cut my face really badly. I'm okay. I'm home now, but I have stitches."

As the story tumbled out of him, I felt my knees weaken. I leaned on the edge of my desk and lowered myself into the chair. My mind was spinning, relieved that Will was okay but furious that no one had called. I felt impotent as a mother, useless and irresponsible. I should have been there. I should have kept calling until I got through. I should have called the police or the hospital earlier.

"I'm so sorry, Will," I said, finding my voice. "I'm

sorry I wasn't there for you, that I didn't speak with you sooner, but I didn't know. Nobody phoned. I only suspected that something had happened because I heard your voice calling me early this morning as I lay in bed."

"Really?" Will exclaimed. Both of us were silent for a moment. Then Will spoke again. "I'm glad you heard me, Mom. Thank you," he said.

"Oh, Will." I wanted to cry but didn't. "I know we're scheduled to see each other this weekend, but I can't wait that long. I think I'll get an earlier flight tomorrow."

"No, Mom." Will was adamant. "Please don't come early. I'm fine, really! I'm even going to school tomorrow."

I paused, hearing the strength in his voice, the certainty in his response. I not only knew that he was probably right, but also that my impulse to fly out immediately was coming more from a deep sense of guilt in me for not having been there for him than from any need of his. Later, lying in bed in Roger's arms, I allowed myself to feel the full extent of my frustration and sorrow. It was painfully clear to me that, having divorced Claude I had also divorced myself from the very real and often unexpected needs of my kids. Huge sobs rose up in me as I fought against a rising wave of despair. Whatever I did, I felt incapable of bridging the tremendous gap between the life and love I wanted to know with my kids and the way things really were.

CHISELS AND WANDS, WORK AND MAGIC

I WALKED SLOWLY UP THE STAIRS to the kitchen where Roger was busy tossing a salad and heating soup for our lunch. As I placed two plates, forks, and knives on the table, I tried to work out what I was going to say to Roger in my head before releasing the words from my mouth.

A month before, a friend had given my book proposal to an agent she knew in New York. Unbelievably to me, the agent, B. G. Dilworth, had called me the next day, saying he loved what I had written and wanted to represent me as an author and show *Hannah's Gift* to publishers. The two of us had worked together to refine the content of the proposal, and a half hour earlier he had called to tell me he was going to send the proposal by messenger to the publishers tomorrow, and he thought I should come to New York immediately in order to meet face-to-face with editors who expressed an interest.

The whole of my life had rushed through me in the brief pause before my response. I had only $700 left in my bank account, the final remnants of my divorce settlement with Claude. I also had no job, no other source of income, and in two weeks, my kids were scheduled to spend the whole summer with me. And yet I also knew that I needed to go to New York. Not only did I trust B.G.'s judgment and experience as an agent, every bone in my body wanted to go.

I felt as if I were riding on the front crest of a wave that had been building since the day I decided to leave my marriage, a movement of life energy that seemed to accelerate once I had committed to writing the book. I trusted this sense I had that I was living in the center of my life. I felt no regrets, no matter what was about to happen. Every penny I had spent in the past year and a half had been consciously spent, and every decision had been thoughtfully made. The sense that I needed to go to New York wasn't something I could rationally explain; it simply felt like the right next thing, arising out of the same assurance I felt that *Hannah's Gift* had a home somewhere, and the publisher it belonged to would know it.

Minutes before, I had told B.G. I would be there, and after hanging up, had called a travel agent and booked the cheapest last-minute flight I could find, $400 round trip from San Francisco to New York with a one-stop layover

Unraveled

in Chicago. Now, seated next to Roger at the kitchen
table, I took a deep breath and let the story pour out.

Roger's eyes widened, and his mouth gaped open.
"Are you crazy? You only have three hundred dollars
left," he said.

Looking at him, I knew that in another time in my
life I might have waffled, thought about canceling the
ticket, changed my mind. But instead, I felt insulated
from his anxiety. I heard his words, knowing that everything he was saying was true while also knowing that
other, more important things were also true. Rather than
feeling impulsive and irresponsible, I felt sure I was doing
the only thing I could do.

My life, my work now was all about chisels and
wands—I would work as hard as I could, like a stone
cutter, cutting through my memories to put words on
the page, getting the proposal to B.G., and flying to New
York. The rest, whatever magic and grace that might
happen out of it, would have to be up to God.

EVERYTHING AND NOTHING THE SAME

I WAS SHAKING AS I picked up the pay phone to make the call. Holding the receiver close to my ear, I listened to the ring over the sounds of the busy airport around me. A man in the booth next to me was arguing with someone. Every thirty seconds, another airline gate attendant made a boarding announcement on the loudspeaker. I barely heard any of it.

Listening to the ring of the phone in my one ear and the airline boarding announcements in the other, I felt strangely lucky, a bit giddy, reckless and wild. A few minutes before, I had called Roger, to let him know I was about to board my flight to San Francisco and to tell him that, although I had no way of knowing yet whether *Hannah's Gift* was going to be published, the five meetings I'd had with publishers had gone well. Roger had sounded breathless when he answered. "Call your agent immediately. You have an offer on your book," he said.

Closing my eyes, I willed B.G. to pick up the phone. When I heard the click of the receiver and then his voice, I let out an audible sigh of relief.

"B.G., it's me, Maria," I said, my heart pounding so loud in my ear, I was afraid I might not hear his response.

"Are you sitting down?" B.G. asked, the excitement in his voice rising. "Bantam has made a preemptive offer of two hundred fifty thousand dollars," he said.

I felt as if I might faint, as my awareness floated out of my body and inside it at the same time. I had been saying yes to my life all these months, trusting that I was doing what my life needed me to do, following my heart in moving to California, and in the writing of my first book. And my life, in this single moment, had turned and said yes to me.

RINGS AND ROSES

IT WAS THE PERFECT first day of the rest of our lives. The sky was clear and covered with stars as country western tunes, played by the Belmont Boys, floated over the bay, and Roger and I danced in each other's arms. Twirling, I caught a glimpse of my parents holding each other close, while Will, Margaret, and Madelaine smiled at everyone and dug deeper into huge pieces of chocolate wedding cake.

The most impossible dreams had finally come true. Earlier in the day, Roger and I had been married on the Bay of San Francisco, by one of our best friends, Palden, a Tibetan lama, under a canopy of ribbons and flowers. I had followed my girls and Will down the aisle, wearing a long, black designer gown, and exchanged vows of love and commitment with the man I adored in front of his mother; my parents, brother, and sister; and thirty of our closest friends.

Unraveled

After the ceremony, I had changed into a rich, gold slip of a dress that Roger had had made for me in Bali, and then everyone had exchanged champagne toasts and tucked into a lovely, catered dinner that our friends Ron and Heidi, whose house we were married in, had generously provided. It was one of those occasions where everyone was smiling and no one wanted to go home. Now, glancing at the thick gold band on my left ring finger, dancing across pink rose petals that Madelaine had sprinkled from her white wicker basket, I smiled into Roger's eyes and could think of nothing more to dream.

ONCE A MOTHER, ALWAYS A MOTHER

I PARKED MY CAR on the shoulder of the road and began the long climb up the side of the mountain, holding the package in my hand. Today, on what would have been Hannah's eleventh birthday, I had received the first galley copy of *Hannah's Gift*. Now, settling into the grass, on the slope of Mt. Tamalpais, overlooking the ocean, I closed my eyes and said a prayer of gratitude for this moment.

I could hardly believe the day had finally come, that my first book, the story of Hannah's life and death, was about to come into the world. Opening my eyes, I carefully pulled the strip along the edge of the package, and pulled the book out. As soon as I saw the image of Hannah's red patent leather shoes on the pure, white cover, I started to cry. Tears streaming down my cheeks, I lay down in the grass and began reading the words that, for months, had poured out of my heart. I felt as if I might explode with pride and amazement, seeing them as I had written them, for the first time, in print, on the page.

My greatest fear, after Hannah's death, had been that she would be forgotten, that her place in my heart would disappear, erode away with the passing of grief and time. But now, as I read, I began to feel Hannah's presence, like a pulsating energy inside my body, a rush of cellular human connection between her and an animal mother love in me. I realized then that Hannah would not only continue to be alive in the pages of this book, she would be alive forever in my bones. And knowing that, I could release her story, like a little paper boat of hope, into the river of the world.

SUMMER IN CORNWALL

THE WOODEN DOOR of the English cottage swung open as Will and his two new friends, twin boys who lived across the path, came in. Dumping their cricket bats and shoes in a pile on the floor, the three boys, laughing and jostling each other, ran upstairs. Smiling, I finished washing the breakfast dishes, and then glanced out the window to check on Margaret and Madelaine, who were playing in the garden.

Roger, the kids, and I had arranged to spend a month in the south of England, in Golant, a small fishing village in Cornwall. After only a week, it already felt like home. Our friends Brian and Deirdre, who had generously offered us the use of their cottage, helped us get acclimated and had already taken us for several sailing excursions on the river. Will had quickly made friends with the boys next door, and now went rowing with them every morning, in sleek, narrow boats. As a family, we had gone sightseeing and explored the neighboring villages, but mostly we had settled into the simplicity of life on the river. Now, even the girls felt comfortable skipping down the hill every afternoon to the pub in town to buy ice cream and bags of "crisps."

Wiping my hands dry on a linen towel, I opened the door to the stone terrace that stretched across the length of the house, affording breathtaking views of the River Fowey below. Roger, who was sitting in a patch of morning sun, reading a book, looked up and smiled. I crossed to him and gave him a kiss. Standing at the edge of the terrace, I inhaled the cool misty air blowing from the southwest, and watched the movement of the river across the landscape.

The river was the life-giving force of this place. Fed by the ocean's tide, it moved slowly, first in one direction, then the other, filling and then draining down to the mud each day. The girls and I loved walking across it once the water had receded, feeling the soft, brown muck squish between our toes, and touching the bottoms of the boats tied to buoys, which were tipped on their sides, waiting patiently for the river to return.

Listening to the excited voices of the boys upstairs, wafting out of an open window, and the girls' quieter murmur rising from the garden, I felt a sense of peace descending on me. *Hannah's Gift* had recently become a

U.K. bestseller and been translated into fifteen foreign languages. And now it seemed that Will, Margaret, Madelaine, and I, along with Roger, were also creating a sense of family and home in a larger, less foreign world.

Unraveled

START WALKING

I WAS IN THE MIDDLE of the strangest dream. A vast sea of faces was turned toward me, each one looking at me with fearful, uncertain eyes. I had a sense that they were the undead, souls that had not yet fully crossed over, and they wanted me to help. Before I could do anything, though, the phone rang, waking me up.

I glanced at the clock before swinging my legs over the side of the bed. It was early, just after 7 A.M. Roger, his eyeshade on and earplugs in, was still sleeping soundly next to me, seemingly undisturbed. The phone was still ringing insistently. I jumped up quickly and answered it. Our friend Jeremiah was breathless on the other end.

"I know you guys don't have a television," he said, his voice cracking as if he was crying. "You'll never believe what's just happened. The East Coast is under attack! Passenger planes have just crashed into the Pentagon and the World Trade Center."

For a split second, I thought I must be dreaming as I struggled to wrap my mind around what Jeremiah had just said. But the racing of my heart and the breathlessness I, too, now felt couldn't be anything but real.

"Oh, my God, my kids are there," I cried out. "I have to get off the phone and call someone," I said, hanging up.

Roger, hearing my shout, sat up, disoriented. "What's wrong?" he said.

I repeated what Jeremiah had said as I frantically dialed the principal's office at the girls' school. The secretary answered on my first ring, and assured me that the children were safe. I told her to call me if there was any change, and then threw on some clothes and told Roger I was going next door to our friends' house to monitor what was happening on television.

All that day, as the images of the Pentagon and World Trade Center smoldered in front of my eyes, I knew only one thing. I had once believed that I could live across the country from my kids, but I believed something very different now. I had to return to them, to the East Coast. If they needed me or I needed them, I wanted to live close enough to simply start walking.

Unraveled

CHRISTMAS WISH

ROGER AND I were sitting on the couch in the apartment in New York City, with Will, Margaret, and Madelaine squished in between us. The tiny Christmas tree we'd purchased from the vendor on the street stood in one corner of the room, festooned with white lights and white paper snowflakes the kids had cut out, and topped with a tinfoil star.

"I have a Christmas surprise for you guys," I said, so excited about telling them, it was all I could do to keep from blurting it out.

"What, what, what?" the three of them shouted.

"Roger and I are moving," I said, drawing the suspense out as long as I could, "We're buying a house, right here, in New York." I was grinning, anticipating their delight. Instead, the three of them were silent, looking at each other, and then at Roger and me.

"Do you mean we won't be living in California anymore?" Will asked quietly. Then he quickly added, "It's not that we're not excited about you living closer to Dad's, it's just that we really liked it there."

I was stunned, truly stunned. I had spent weeks, since September 11, playing the scene over and over in my mind, imagining all three kids crying with happiness and relief, knowing Roger and I would be living just down the road. Now I realized it was my guilt as a mother that had staged the scene I imagined. The truth was, while it hadn't been easy for any of us to be living so far apart, it hadn't been at all as difficult as I had believed either.

"It *will* be fun to live closer to each other, Mom," Margaret said finally, giving me a hug.

"Yeah," Will said, smiling now. "I have to admit, I was hoping you'd stay in California for at least a couple more years. The legal driving age there is sixteen, and here in New Jersey it's a year later. I was really looking forward to having my license before all of my friends."

Madelaine, who had been silent until now, leaned over and gave me a kiss. "It's okay that you're moving to New York, Mommy," she said. "Besides, you always did tell us, 'Momma always comes back.' "

Unraveled

TOUGH LOVE

I PULLED MY car into Claude's driveway and checked the clock. I was five minutes early. I shut off the engine, unbuckled my seat belt, and opened the door. Approaching the house, I realized some part of me still felt as if I lived there, even though it had been more than five years since the divorce. So many of the memories still alive in me had been made in this place, especially my memories of Hannah, whose spirit, eight and a half years later, could sometimes seem like a good idea I once had, rather than the little girl I'd do anything for. She was here, along with traces of the woman I once was, imbued in every surface in the house, every brick in the sidewalk, and every blade of grass on the lawn.

Peeking through the window into the entry hall, I rang the front doorbell. I could see the gold-framed mirror and welcome sign in the same place where I'd hung them when we had first moved in. Although Claude had not allowed me inside since our divorce was final, I knew that some things had changed. From the kids, I knew that there was now a computer in the living room, and the nursery-playroom had been converted to a bedroom for the au pair.

Margaret came running to the door and opened it. "Hi, Mom!" she said, throwing her arms around me. "We're just finishing packing our stuff. We'll be right out."

"Okay, no hurry," I said, smiling. "I'll wait."

Returning to the car, I leaned back in the front seat. Just then I heard a loud roar as Claude, pushing the lawn mower, came around the corner of the house. I smiled and felt my heart do a somersault. I still felt a deep affection for him, as impossible as it might seem. More than anything, right now, I wanted to be able to jump out of the car, run up to him, and say hello. I could even imagine him shutting the lawn mower off for a moment, so we could have a conversation, catch up on each other's lives, while I waited for the kids.

But none of this was possible, and I knew it. Claude still hadn't spoken a single word to me, on the phone or in person, for more than four years, refusing even to look at me when we crossed paths. For a long time, I had implored him, via e-mail and letter, to consider how harmful his behavior toward me was for our kids. But I had gradually understood that the more I pushed to engage him, the more I was playing into the damaging dynamics between us. I began to suspect that his silence was an attempt to freeze things between us in order to keep them, like the house, forever what they were.

But I was no longer who I was, although some traces still remained. Almost forty years old, now, my sense of self was less dependent on the actions and beliefs of others in my life. I had turned a corner, somewhere along the line, and knew that my life was now all about permission— permission to be imperfect, to make mistakes, to be afraid. And in giving myself permission to be and experience all these things, I was also able to grant the same permission to those I loved. For me, life was no longer about being "good"; it was about being true.

Watching Claude pushing the lawn mower back and forth across the front yard, his brow creased in concentration or perhaps in an effort to ignore me, I knew I could not change how he chose to behave. But I *could* choose how to deal with it. Rather than needing to embarrass him or shame him or make him wrong, I chose to see him as a human being, like me: imperfect, struggling, and learning. And seeing that, I also chose to continue to love and respect him for what we had once shared together, for being the father of the children we both loved. Though I would never give up hope that things might eventually ease between us, I could be at peace with the way it was, knowing that loving fully *really does* mean letting go.

BREATHING INTO THE VOID

I PICKED MY WAY carefully through the living room on my way to the kitchen, smiling at the chaos. Every piece of furniture had been haphazardly rearranged and draped with sheets and blankets. A handmade sign reading, "Privisy Please. No boys aloud" was taped to the door of the fort. Margaret and Madelaine, huddled underneath, giggled as I passed.

Moments later, Madelaine crawled out of her hiding place and joined me as I sat on the porch, sipping my coffee. Settling herself into my lap, she rested her head against my chest. The two of us sat silently, rocking and looking out over the trees.

"Mommy, I want you to come to my baseball game next Saturday," Madelaine said quietly, turning her head to look into my eyes.

I smiled at her. "Of course, honey," I replied, kissing the top of her head. "I wouldn't miss it."

"But Mommy," she said, sitting up, "I don't know

where the game is going to be, and Daddy won't tell me because he doesn't want you to come."

I felt my heart clench in my chest and tried not to let my face register my anger. Claude's continued rejection of me was a reality the children and I were learning to live with, but it wasn't easy. There were times, like now, when I wanted nothing more than to track him down and shake or shout the selfishness out of him. I knew that his behavior, no matter the justification, hurt Will, Margaret, and Madelaine more than it could ever hurt me.

Margaret, having overheard the conversation through the open door, crawled out of the fort and joined us on the porch. Reaching for her, I pulled her onto my lap next to Madelaine. The three of us rocked quietly. A hummingbird skimmed toward us and paused, its tiny wings whirring, while I collected my thoughts before answering.

"I'm sorry, Madelaine," I said finally. "I can't imagine how hard this must be for you. But while this is clearly the way Daddy wants to handle it, we don't have to let it stop us from doing what is the best, right thing for you. I wonder if there's another way we can handle it."

"I know," said Margaret excitedly, sitting up quickly in my lap. "Why don't we call one of the other kids on Maddy's team and ask where the game is!"

"Yes!" Madelaine exclaimed. Her face and mine broke into wide smiles as the three of us beamed at each other. Then the two of them scrambled out of my arms and disappeared into the house.

Staring into the trees, I took a sip of my coffee and felt grateful for the simplicity with which we had once again managed to sidestep a painful confrontation with Claude. I couldn't help thinking it was all the more perfect that the girls themselves had come up with the solution. And I now understood that my willingness to be creative and resourceful in dealing with Claude's emotional short-comings rather than getting more and more frustrated, waiting for him to change, was helping my children learn to do the same thing.

Unraveled

LOG CABIN

I CLEARED THE PAPER-PLATE puppets off the
picnic table on the back porch, and then called to the
girls, who were building a tepee out of branches they
had dragged out of the woods into the backyard.

"It's time to get ready for your art lesson," I said.

"Okay, Mom, we're coming," they called back.

It was summer, and we were now living in New York,
in a log cabin perched on the shoulder of a mountain,
just outside Woodstock. Bare, stripped logs, each once a
tree, had been stacked and fitted together to make our
home. A huge stone fireplace and woodstove stood in the
living room, and two long porches stretched along the
front and back of the house. Will and the girls spent their
weekends and summers roaming the woods, collecting
tiny newts and building forts. Sometimes the four of us
pulled Roger away from his writing studio, and the five
of us would walk down the hill to visit with neighbors or
wade and fish in the stream.

Now, standing on the dirt road at the end of our drive, wearing faded Levi's, one of my dad's old work shirts, and a pair of lapis earrings from Morocco, my hair pulled back into a ponytail, I watched the girls skipping down the hill toward Ted, our friend and neighbor, who was also a retired filmmaker and part-time artist. Days before, Margaret had spotted him painting a picture on an easel in his front yard and boldly asked him to give her and Madelaine art lessons. Smiling, he had agreed.

Watching the girls now, holding Ted's hands, waving to me as they disappeared around the bend, I suddenly felt overwhelmed by a sense of déjà vu. I realized then, in that moment, that my life had finally come full circle from the day I had walked to the end of the dirt road at the retreat center and slid my postcards into the mailbox. I was finally the woman I had always believed I could be, a wife and mother, fully in her life, watching her daughters fully in theirs.

My life now felt as incomplete and perfect as a mother's day when everyone is safe and asleep but there is still a load of laundry in the dryer as she climbs into bed. I was at peace with the gap between who I was and what I knew, and willing to accept that while I knew a great many things, I was still so few of them. I also had no need right now to pretend that I was a part-time mom wishing I were a full-time one. Although in my heart I fully expected that one day I would return again to being a mother in the everyday sense of the word, for now I loved that the flexibility I had as a writer, combined with our custody arrangement, afforded me space and solitude in which to work during the school year, when the kids lived with Claude, and then allowed me to give Will, Margaret, and Madelaine my full attention when I was with them.

And while Roger's love for me and for my children was a part of the peace I now experienced in my life, I was no longer interested in having a perfect life or a perfect marriage. I understood that the struggles and challenges of a relationship are an inherent part of the package, and that the heart of a good marriage is the love that sustains it and that allows us, individually and separately, to grow. My husband's darkness and my own were things I was still learning to fall in love with, and more and more, I was also learning to trust what my imperfections could teach me.

And while I was still certain I had made the right decision in divorcing Claude, I knew that I might never know for sure whether I done the right thing in giving him primary custody of our children. Everything looks different when we turn around and see all those abandoned campsites, those people we once were. But what I did trust, without question, as I turned and strolled back to the cabin, was that what I had said to Will alongside that campfire in Kansas more than four years before was still true: who I was and what I knew was constantly changing, but the love I felt for my children, for Roger, and even for Claude was solid, unwavering. It was the best of who I was.

Epilogue

L a   M è r e   (The Mother),
L a   M e r   (The Sea)

AS I WRITE THESE WORDS, the epilogue of this book, it is important to me that you, the reader, know that Roger and I, still married and in love, now own two places: his, a sweet one-bedroom in the West Village of Manhattan, and mine, a condominium across the river from the apartment where I lived the first year after my divorce. Taking the ferry back and forth, we live our lives separately and together. But more important, I have finally returned to my rightful place by my kids and the sea.

Not long ago, as Roger and I left a theater in New York City, I received a phone call from Madelaine, who is now eight years old. As I stood in the middle of a busy sidewalk in Manhattan, my cell phone pressed against my ear, listening to her play a piano piece she intended to perform at her recital, the bittersweetness of the moment was not lost on me. I have given up more than I ever imagined I would have to give in order to live this life that I know, without a doubt, is mine. There are many days when my heart still aches to be more with my kids, but I also know and trust that I am close to and still discovering my changes.

And each morning as I sit on my terrace, sipping my coffee and gazing out at the ocean, I feel blessed to be reminded again that every river, no matter its twists and bends, always returns to the sea."

ACKNOWLEDGMENTS

EVERY LIFE OWES A DEBT of gratitude to those who either willingly or unwittingly offer themselves to it. Mine is no different. To Roger Housden, my beloved husband; to Will, Hannah, Margaret, and Madelaine, my cherished children; and to countless friends, teachers, family members, and guides: My faith is stronger and my heart softer because of your presence in my life and I am grateful.

ABOUT THE AUTHOR

MARIA HOUSDEN is an author and lecturer. She and her husband, Roger, live in New York and New Jersey. Her first book, *Hannah's Gift: Lessons From a Life Fully Lived,* was published in 2001 and has become an international bestseller, translated into more than 15 foreign languages. Maria is currently launching an ambitious global initiative called GRIEF IN ACTION. You can read more about her and her work on her website, www.hannahsgift.com.